THE LIFE HISTORY
METHOD

THE LIFE HISTORY METHOD

Studying People of African Descent

OHENE ANIWA
(KING'S EYES)

BEAUTY, VIGILANCE

The king's eyes. A symbol of vigilance, far-sightedness, intelligence, protection, security, defence, authority, and power. From the aphorism, "Ohene aniwa twa ne ho hyia," to wit, "The kings eyes surround him," that is, "The king sees everything."

THE LIFE HISTORY METHOD

Studying People of African Descent

Doris Kakuru, PhD

Little Black Book Series

RESEARCH METHODOLOGY, THEORY, AND PRAXIS

Volume 3

Universal Write Publications, LLC
New York, NY

THE LIFE HISTORY METHOD: STUDYING PEOPLE OF AFRICAN
DESCENT

Copyright © 2025 by Universal Write Publications, LLC

Library of Congress Control Number: 2025916348

PRINT: ISBN: 978-1-942774-53-2
eBOOK: ISBN: 978-1-942774-52-5

Printed in the United States of America.

Mailing/Submissions:

Universal Write Publications, LLC
421 8th avenue, Suite 86
New York, NY 10116

Website: UWPBooks.com

This book has been partially supported with a financial grant from
SAGE Publishing.

Dedication

To my mother, Ferestas, and my grandmother, Peresika. May your love, guidance, and sacrifices be honored in these pages. This book is your harvest and legacy.

Acknowledgments

I acknowledge the mentorship of D. Josephine Etowa, whose wisdom has shaped my thinking and practice over the years. I am grateful to Dr. Shemine Gulamhusein, Leslie Prpich, Jshandeep Jassal, Leonard Misana, and Trinity Schlitz for the various ways in which you contributed to this book. I am especially thankful to my colleagues Dr. Mandeep Kaur Mucina, Dr. Sandrina Carere, and Shanne McCaffery and many others for your friendship, understanding, and care. To the UWP team especially Little Black Book Series Editor Dr. Serie McDougal III and Dr. Ayo Sekai, thank you for your patience and for the opportunity to collaborate on this book.

To members of the Black community and to my research participants worldwide: your powerful stories have been a profound source of inspiration. I write in recognition of the enduring afterlives of slavery and the continuing harms borne by Black peoples; any insight in these pages is indebted to your resilience.

To my students over the past two decades, I have learned invaluable lessons from our interactions, and I am grateful that our paths crossed. I also acknowledge the many scholars whose work informs this book.

To my huge family in Ottawa and across the globe; I thank God for you! You have often borne my absences with grace and understanding. I honor my ancestors, community elders, and spiritual leaders whose timeless teachings continue to guide me.

Contents

List of Tables

List of Figures

CHAPTER 1

Understanding Life History Research

*... Then I grew older and began to read about adventures in which I didn't know that I was supposed to be on the side of those savages who were encountered by the good white man. I instinctively took sides with the white people. They were fine! They were excellent. They were intelligent. The others were not ... they were stupid and ugly. That was the way I was introduced to the danger of not having your own stories. There is that great [African] proverb—**that until the lions have their own historians, the history of the hunt will always glorify the hunter**. That did not come to me until much later. Once I realized that, I had to be a writer. I had to be that historian. It's not one man's job. It's not one person's job. But it is something we have to do, so that the story of the hunt will also reflect the agony, the travail—the bravery, even, of the lions.*

(Chinua Achebe as cited in Brooks, 1994, para 8–9)

INTRODUCTION

While growing up in Uganda, I loved listening to adults' stories. I was particularly intrigued by my grandmother's stories, and I often listened in to my mother's conversations with her friends and with her mother (my grandmother). My grandmother also told my siblings and me many stories about her life experience as a child and later as a mother and wife. She particularly spoke of people I had never met, ancestors whose names rolled off her tongue like poetry. She told me about the seasons when the rains came early, or late, and her experience with forced marriage. She narrated the struggles she faced educating my mother during the colonial era, and how her quiet resistance defied patriarchal expectations in ways that seemed small but were, in fact, seismic. My grandmother did not have an opportunity to go to school. She learned how to read and write from her church. She grew up in a culture that prioritized sending boys to school and marrying off girls. She got married at the age of 14. She was motivated to send her two children to school because to her, education opened the opportunity of formal employment. She thought that if she had been educated, she would have been empowered enough at least to choose her own spouse. However, my grandfather (her husband) was not in support of formal education. My grand-mother had to find her own ways of getting money to send her two kids to school. My mother attended a boarding secondary school in the 1950s that was the only one in the entire district at the time. She needed money for tuition fees and other require-ments, including transport. My grandmother's only income was from selling animal products such as milk and ghee. Although she was required to hand over all the money to her husband at the end of the day, she discreetly kept some of it. This money would eventually add up and be spent on the educational needs of her daughter—my mother. That is how my mother went through education to become a schoolteacher. My grandmoth-er's stories of resilience and determination inspired me to be what I am today. My grandmother's experience was not unique to her. Many of her peers faced similar, if not worse, injustices and overcame them (Kanogo, 2005; Lykes, 1983). During colo-nial times, people of African descent, whether in Africa or in other locations around the world where their ancestors had been enslaved, exercised agency, and overcame oppression from governmental and patriarchal authorities. My grandmother's stories were living, breathing accounts of resilience, survival, joy, and the everyday negotiations of life under oppressive societal structures and norms. However, such stories of resilience and agency were not given due attention in textbooks and scholarly literature—they did not fit neatly into the timelines or textbooks I would later study in school.

Black people and people of African descent are of different kinds. They are a heterogeneous demographic whose ancestry can be traced back to sub-Saharan Africa (Jean-Pierre et al., 2024). The history of research on Black people and people of African descent is complex and often problematic. According to Breasted (1920), Egypt was the first region where structured systems of governance, and education emerged, a process later described by colonial powers as "civilization." Historical evidence suggests that the first successful Cesarean section was performed in Uganda long before modern Western medical advancements. Despite this rich history, people of African descent continue to be labeled as backward and underdeveloped. Colonial anthropologists often reinforced stereotypes of primitiveness and tribalism (Pierre, 2020). Pierre explains how colonial anthropological literature frequently ignored the profound impacts of the role played by race in the transatlantic slave trade and colonialism. Unethical historical research practices, such as the Tuskegee Syphilis Study, have significantly contributed to the deep-seated mistrust of research within Black communities (Awidi & Al Hadidi, 2021; Corbie-Smith et al., 2002). Research with Black communities has often been marked by unequal power dynamics, with many studies conducted by researchers who prioritized their own agendas and methods over the perspectives of the communities being studied (Hafkin & Bay, 1976; Smaw, 2022). According to Hafkin and Bay (1976),

Black people are frequently relegated to the role of research subjects, "informants," or assistants with little control over the research agenda or outcomes. This practice masks the agency of people of African descent because deficit narratives are prioritized, some of which violate ritual and customary traditions for describing a people. Research was often driven by colonial interests, such as understanding local customs and traditions to fuel the colonization agenda. This led to a focus on research that reinforced colonial narratives and justified colonial rule.

When I studied anthropology in graduate school and was introduced to the life history research method, it reminded me of my grandmother's stories. However, it was when I found myself in North America that the power of storytelling, especially among Black people, took on new meaning. I realized that the stories about Black people and people of African descent were fractured, disrupted by forced migrations, anti-Black racism, colonial legacies, and the silences that came from both trauma and resilience. I recognized that, like my grandmother's stories, the lives of people of African descent need to be recorded with care, not just as historical facts, but as narratives that reveal the depth of who they are, how they move through the world, and how they make sense of their experiences. George Floyd's murder by a white police officer in 2020 spearheaded the rise of anti-racist research initiatives, and many researchers began studying Black communities without adequate preparation or cultural awareness, increasing the importance of rethinking how to conduct ethical and culturally responsive research among Black diasporic communities (Jean-Pierre et al., 2024, 2025).

As a Black, cisgender, neurotypical, able-bodied Canadian African immigrant woman who has had access to education, I recognize that my perspective is shaped by both privilege and marginalization. My life experiences as a scholar who migrated to North America with three Black teenage sons at the time of

George Floyd's murder and the ensuing Black Lives Matter movement shape the work I do, including this book.

WHY THIS BOOK

The Black Lives Matter movement highlighted the urgent need for reform and justice, and it has led to numerous studies and publications addressing anti-Black racism. However, not everyone is well equipped with the tools to conduct emancipatory research in a culturally sensitive manner. This book is an effort to provide such tools. I write from the understanding that the stories of people of African descent around the world deserve to be told in ways that honor our complexities and truths.

The ideas shared in this book are rooted in the tradition of Africana and African studies, a broad, interdisciplinary field that explores the histories, cultures, and experiences of people across the African diaspora, encompassing regions in North America, South America, the Caribbean, and the African continent (Conyers, 1997). The field emerged in response to the historical marginalization of Black voices and perspectives within mainstream academia. It seeks to address the complex issues of race, identity, and social justice. The origins of Africana Studies can be traced back to the broader struggles for racial equality and the Civil Rights Movement in the United States during the mid-20th century (Rojas, 2007). The need for academic discourse that reflected the realities and contributions of Black people became apparent when traditional academic narratives largely excluded or misrepresented African and African diasporic histories. In the 1960s, college students and Black intellectuals demanded the establishment of academic programs that would address these discrepancies. This led to the institution of Black Studies programs across universities, which later evolved into the more encompassing Africana studies. While the social sciences often aim to generate knowledge across diverse societies and aim to equip graduates with research skills and tools needed to study all communities, Black and Africana studies focus on distinctive features of Black culture, histories, and experiences, which sometimes require unique methodological approaches (Rojas, 2007).

Scholars of Black and Africana studies must recognize the plurality of Black ethnicities, cultures, experiences, histories, and futures. Previous work about how to conduct life history research has focused on specific disciplines such as education (Gomez et al., 2015; Goodson, 2012), psychology (Kaplan & Gangestad, 2015), and nursing (De Chesnay, 2014). This book describes the techniques and practical aspects of conducting and communicating life history research to various audiences concerned with decolonizing research methodologies. It covers the research process, including sample selection, data collection methods, data analysis, and knowledge mobilization strategies. The book is also about how to conduct life history research with people of African descent in a way that centers their voices, ways of knowing, diversity, and the nuances of their lived experiences. It is about ensuring that the histories and experiences of Black communities, like my grandmother's stories, do not fade into silence but instead shape the futures we are building on this planet.

Now that you have an idea why a book about how to conduct research with Black people and people of African descent is important, let us move on to why you might want to use the life history research method.

What is Life History Research?

The life history method is a qualitative research method used to collect and analyze detailed personal histories. It seeks to uncover the complexities of individuals' experiences over time. It focuses on capturing the longitudinal cycles, rhythms, and changes that characterize a person's life. Using the life history method to collect personal narratives allows for a better understanding of how individuals have arrived at their current life circumstances. This approach connects personal stories to broader social, political, and cultural contexts relevant to the research topic (Plaza, 2006). By embracing the principle of *sankofa*, narratives of Black people reveal how they retrieve and make sense of their past experiences, cultural heritage, and ancestral knowledge to inform their present and future. Sankofa is a West African concept that emphasizes the importance of learning from the past, honoring one's heritage, and retrieving valuable knowledge and wisdom that has been lost or forgotten. When applied to research, this retrospective gaze enables researchers to gain a deeper understanding of the complex interplay between individual agency and structural factors that shape Black people's life experiences. Unlike research methods that solicit participants' opinions and analyze them to create a coherent linear story that would appeal to the researcher's readers, the life history method is empowering. It prioritizes "experiences of individuals across time from [their] own perspective and voice" (Pabon, 2017, p. 773). Life history becomes the most feasible approach to give insights into the complexities between one's historical experience and the broader social and cultural contexts (Goodson, 2001).

Life history as a research method began in the 19th century but became prominent in the 20th century among the sociologists in the Chicago School. Early anthropologists used life history as part of their ethnographic research approach to study tribal cultures and societies mainly outside of Europe. In the 1800s, such societies were inhabited by Indigenous peoples who were described in anthropological literature as "non-industrialized" or "primitive" (Etienne & Leacock, 1980). According to Clifford (1986), early anthropologists, who were mainly Europeans, were more interested in "discovering cultures" than providing adequate representations and explanations of culture. The ethnographer entered a community as the holder of epistemic power (Fricker, 2007). They imposed their own biases and assumptions on their research participants, who were often people of color from colonized or Indigenous communities. Influenced by their prejudices about the cultures they studied, researchers typically conducted participant observation and collected life stories. They assumed the authority of research expertise and owned the knowledge of the societies they studied and the conclusions they drew. Research participants had little control over how their cultures and communities were represented in research findings. This white supremacy violated the epistemic agency (Dotson, 2014) of the local knowers or study participants. Life history is, therefore, a research method that originated from anthropological studies of people who had not been previously studied. However, unlike some qualitative research methods where the researcher collects data, interprets them, and draws conclusions based on the expertise of the research participants, the life history can be more liberating. It attaches value to a person's own story and the interpretations study participants place on their own experience as an explanation of behavior (Kakuru & Paradza, 2007).

In the years before 1970, ethnographic research was considered a low-status research approach (Antikainen, 2016; Denzin, 1992). Due to the popularity of objectivism and positivist science, the use of life histories as sources of empirical data was criticized (Antikainen, 2016). The rise of symbolic interactionism fueled scholars' interest in analyzing societal and human interactions and not individuals' experiences or life stories. However, during the postmodern era with the associated impact of modernization, societies became increasingly individualized, and suddenly there was a realization and recognition of the importance of subjectivism in research. Hence, as the individualization of society increased, the need to analyze individual experiences and life stories became more apparent. Currently, life history has revitalized its space in science research due to increased postmodern valuing of subjectivity and personal narratives as the doors to understanding social realities (Goodson, 2016). The research landscape has therefore been characterized by a consistent shift from grand narratives to small-scale personal narratives and a wide acceptance of individual experiences and the subjective nature of truth making. This shift makes the life history an excellent method for conducting identity-related research (Goodson, 2001; Goodson et al., 2016).

However, research on Black people has always been rooted in Western ways of knowing, knowledge production, and understanding the world (Osei-Tutu, 2021a). Although Black communities and individuals exhibit remarkable plurality and diversity and Black ontologies encompass a wide range of experiences and perspectives, the life history method has traditionally been applied to the study of Black people and people of African descent based on an oversimplified and flawed notion of a monolithic Black demographic.

As a demographic whose ancestors were enslaved, colonized, and framed as primitive by early researchers (see Franz, 1986; Talal, 1979), Afro-descendant people have endured such oppressive labels and research methodologies that violated their epistemic justice as knowers. Contemporary researchers must challenge and change rigid and dominant research norms and promote a more inclusive and nuanced approach to understanding diasporic Black people's experiences. Decolonizing life history research with Black people and people of African descent is crucial. Equally important is acquiring the necessary skills and knowledge to do so effectively.

Advantages of Life History Method to Study Black People

At the core of life history methods are human narratives, which foster the four urgencies of "speaking, being heard, collective stories, and urgency of public stories" (Denzin & Lincoln, 2011, p. 427). By *urgency of speaking*, Denzin and Lincoln (2011) mean giving power to narrators to provide accounts of their life experiences they perceive worthy of telling. The *urgency of being heard* is when one's story is made available for other people to hear it, while *collective stories* refers to more pronounced life stories about social justice practices in which the story of a single person connects to a broader social group of people with similar experiences, such as individual stories from refugees or sexually abused children and women, for example. Lastly, *the urgency of public dialogue*, according to the authors, is when people's life accounts can inform public issues (Denzin & Lincoln, 2011). In Black and Africana studies, using the life history method to research Black people and people of African descent offers various advantages, as outlined below.

Narrowing the Power Gap

In both quantitative and qualitative research, researchers typically take time to design the study and plan its implementation. They think through the data collection tools and pilot them, go through the process of obtaining consent and meeting ethics board requirements, and by the time they go to the field, they are mentally prepared to engage with the participants. Researchers prepare this way because their role as researcher comes with power. The participant, on the other hand, is rarely given an opportunity to plan. In many research studies, participants are recruited and given an appointment for an interview without much preparation. In the life history method, data collection can involve a series of visits. Even when the researcher initiates the process, the participant sets the pace at which the story is narrated. It has thus been applauded for narrowing the power gap in research through bringing the researcher and the participant into the same "emotional space" (Kakuru & Paradza, 2007, p. 289).

The emotional depth and personal struggles of Black people, which are often obscured by statistical analyses, are preserved through life history research, providing a rich and nuanced understanding of the past. Spooner (2019) described how the life history method allowed Indigenous experiences to be centered, resistance to colonial erasure to be documented, and the role of place in shaping identity and collective memory to be reimagined. Offering marginalized communities an opportunity to detail their experiences, inform theory, and expand existing knowledge is often missing from research that values statistics over lived experience to approach analysis (Kouritzin, 2000). By uncovering overlooked narratives, life history research produces inclusive discourse. Life history research thus provides a platform for personal narratives for those who might otherwise be sidelined by broad generalizations and exclusionary research practices (Lanford et al., 2019).

Offering a Comfortable Research Environment

The rich oral traditions of Black communities characterized by the transmission of stories, wisdom, and historical knowledge through spoken word rather than written records present a significant opportunity for life history research. By utilizing a storytelling format that aligns with participants' cultural heritage, life history research fosters a comfortable research environment. The life history method creates a safe space for participants to freely express themselves without reservation.

Capturing the Depth of Personal and Generational Experiences

Afrocentric storytelling practices such as "by the fireside" (Osei-Tutu, 2021b) and values such as *ubuntu* (Mbiti, 1969; Mucina, 2011) enhance the "thickness" of the narratives produced, yielding detailed and reflective insights of the participants' experiences. One of the primary strengths of life history research, particularly for people of African descent, lies in its capacity to elucidate the complexities of identity formation and generational migration and postmigration experiences. In Black diasporic communities, certain racialized experiences may be underreported in other research approaches because they are perceived as normalized (Osei-Tutu, 2023). By tracing entire life trajectories, life history research reveals long-term patterns of racialization, cultural adaptation, and social mobility, thereby providing a nuanced understanding of the intersections between individual agency and structural forces. The narrative inquiry approach (Clandinin, 2022) to life history research enables participants to construct their own stories, ensuring that their lived experiences are represented accurately. This is particularly significant for diasporic Black people whose life experiences have been shaped by the legacy of slavery and the erasure of their stories from dominant historical narratives. By situating individual narratives within the broader historical and social contexts that shape them and counteracting deficit-based narratives, life history research qualifies as a powerful method for understanding the intricacies of Black communities. According to Plaza (2006), the life history method offers rich data on Black people's perspectives on life as well as on their sociocultural values and social norms.

Flexible Data Collection

The life history method is a flexible data collection approach. Researchers can incorporate personal letters, photographs, and even artistic expressions (music, poetry, artifacts) to deepen the storytelling process. Visual methods of data collection can enhance qualitative research by providing a unique window into complex social realities, allowing researchers to access and convey meanings and experiences that might be difficult to capture through spoken or written language alone (Pincock & Jones, 2020). The flexibility of the life history method offers researchers an opportunity to dismantle conventional Euro-Western and colonial ways of data collection. In their study about African, Caribbean, and Black young adults who have immigrated to Canada, Myrie et al. (2022) created a research environment that they believe challenged the normative Western social science interview. The flexibility of the life history method offers the researcher "room to think," which is important in research about Black communities.

The adaptability of life history research to a variety of disciplines and research topics demonstrates its flexibility and relevance in investigating complex human experiences. It has been applied in Black/Africana studies (Myrie et al., 2022; Lane, 2016; Osseo-Asare, 2017; Stitt & Happel-Parkins, 2019), African studies (Boonzaier & Van Schalkwyk, 2011; Kakuru & Paradza, 2007; Van Niekerk & Boonzaier, 2019), sociology (Catherine Corrigall–Brown et al., 2013), anthropology (Edgar, 2009; Leone et al., 2005; Lane, 2016; Rebecca Sear & Sear, 2020), educational research (Gomez et al., 2015; Goodson & Sikes, 2016; Osseo-Asare, 2017; Samuel, 2009), public health (De Chesnay, 2014; Kakuru et al., 2024; Luebbert & Amelia Perez, 2016; Magnan et al., 2023; Smith, 2015; Yoshihama et al., 2006), psychology (Kaplan & Gangestad, 2015; Myrie et al., 2022), and other fields. The life history method is valued for helping researchers in various disciplines integrate personal narratives with broader theoretical frameworks to understand identity and social structures across diverse fields of study.

LIFE HISTORY RESEARCH PHILOSOPHY

Philosophy in research refers to the abstract ideas and beliefs on which our research decisions are based. Research philosophy can therefore be described as the application of rational, critical, and logical thinking in the research process (Creswell & Poth, 2024). It concerns our beliefs about the research process and how these beliefs influence the choice of the research methodology—how we do research. Philosophical assumptions also help us to identify the theoretical and interpretive frameworks, evaluate the different research methodologies and approaches, and make decisions about how to collect, analyze, and report data.

Ontology and Epistemology

Ontology and epistemology are two fundamental concepts in research that inform the choices we make about what we study and the methods we use to study those things. *Ontology* is the study of being. It can be described as the nature of reality that we seek to understand. It asks questions as follows: What is truth? In what form does truth exist? What is the nature of existence? For example, many would agree that obesity is a health condition. However, ontologically, one would wonder whether obesity is solely a biological health condition or a condition influenced by societal factors like food marketing and affordability and sociocultural norms. This is an ontological debate surrounding obesity questioning whether it is an inherent medical issue or a condition shaped by external social and environmental determinants. What is the truth about obesity? This debate is about whether obesity exists independently or is shaped by factors outside of the individual. What is the truth about obesity? How do we understand it? If it is shaped by factors outside of the individual, then what is the best way to investigate obesity? Black people and people of African descent have their own unique ontologies, which emphasize ancestral heritage, spirituality, and community. Black ontologies are shaped by Afrocentric practices and philosophies.

Examples of Black Ontologies

Sankofa, a philosophical principle that acknowledges the importance of history and heritage, underpins the sacredness of life history data. Sankofa is a powerful symbol and concept from West Africa that is often represented by a bird that looks backward while moving forward. It represents a philosophical approach that speaks to the importance of learning from the past, honoring one's heritage, and retrieving valuable knowledge and wisdom that has been lost or forgotten (Jean-Pierre et al., 2024). Jean-Pierre et al. (2024) note that Black Canadians practice sankofa in their narratives.

Ubuntu is another example of Black ontologies made popular by Mbiti (1969). Black communities globally believe in the ubuntu philosophy, which is a South African moral system that means "I am because we are, and because we are, therefore I am" (Ewuoso & Hall, 2019; Gathogo, 2022; Jean-Pierre et al., 2024; Mbiti, 1969; Mucina, 2011). Ubuntu honors the interconnectedness of members of the Black community as a group rather than isolated individuals (White, 2025). To Black people and people of African descent, individual knowledge is community knowledge. By incorporating Mbiti's concept of ubuntu into the life history method, researchers can gain a deeper understanding of Black people's experiences and the ways in which community, interconnectedness, and relationships shape their lives.

Nommo is a concept that originates from African philosophy, particularly from the Dogon people of Mali, and refers to the power of the spoken word to create, shape, and transform reality (Cummings & Roy, 2002; Howard, 2011). Nommo evolved in the 1960s as a framework for understanding African American rhetorical practices and communicative practices in general. It was made popular by Asante (1998), who linked it to Afrocentricity and the oral traditions of Africans brought to America. Asante argued that diasporic Black people's communicative practices are rooted in their African heritage. He argued that nommo continues to permeate our existence and that any scholar "who undertakes an analysis of the [B] lack past without recognizing the significance of vocal expression as a transforming agent is treading on intellectual quicksand" (Asante, 2004, p. 17). Black communication has unique features like rhythm, call-and-response, and improvisation that are rooted in Afrocentric oral traditions such as nommo. In many African and African diasporic traditions, speech is not just communication; it is a force with spiritual, social, and political power. Nommo emphasizes that words are not neutral—they can heal, empower, curse, and manifest change (Cummings & Roy, 2002). Nommo aligns with the African oral tradition, where storytelling, naming, proverbs, and praise poetry serve as tools for both resistance and knowledge transmission (Howard, 2011; Karenga, 2014). Nommo is therefore an Afrocentric ontology. In the context of Afrocentric research and Black life history analysis, nommo suggests that stories of Black people and people of African descent must be understood within their cultural and epistemological context. And not all stories are told the way non-Blacks understand storying. For example, names of places and people can hold significant meaning and tell stories that may not be immediately apparent. In many African cultures, names are often imbued with profound meaning, reflecting the circumstances of a child's birth, including their birthplace, birth time, family lineage, and cultural or spiritual heritage.

Some Black people's names are deeply connected to the circumstances of the person's birth, reflecting the social, cultural, or environmental context of the time. These names can serve as a form of storytelling, capturing significant events, conditions, or experiences that were present at the moment of birth.[1] Examples of such names might include those referencing:

---

[1] The name Kakuru, for example, holds significant cultural meaning. It specifically indicates that the person bearing this name is the first-born twin. There is a distinct name for the second-born twin as a traditional naming practice.

- the location or circumstances of birth (e.g., on the way to the hospital)
- seasonal or environmental conditions (e.g., born during a time of plenty or scarcity)
- significant events or cultural practices (e.g., born during a time of celebration or conflict).

Such names not only provide a sense of identity and belonging but also serve as a connection to one's heritage and community. They can also offer a unique perspective on historical events, cultural traditions, and the experiences of individuals and communities. Therefore, as a researcher, it is essential to be mindful of the language and terminology one uses, especially when working with diverse Black cultures and communities. The term *family name*, for example, is not universally applicable, as not all Black families share a common name. This highlights the importance of cultural sensitivity and awareness in research. It is also crucial to recognize that stories and information can be conveyed in various ways, not just through spoken words. Some stories might be embedded in names, traditions, or cultural practices, requiring researchers to be attentive to these nuances. By being aware of these complexities, researchers can approach their work with a more nuanced understanding, avoiding assumptions and misinterpretations that might arise from cultural insensitivity or a lack of awareness.

In Black communities, understanding nommo is crucial because it acknowledges that reality encompasses a multifaceted array of expressions and communications. These include not only spoken words, such as verbal storytelling and conversations, but also unspoken expressions like nonverbal cues and body language. Additionally, nommo recognizes the significance of actions, including behaviors, rituals, and practices that convey meaning, as well as nonactions, such as deliberate silences, omissions, or withholding of information, that also convey meaning. By embracing this nuanced understanding of nommo, researchers can approach interactions with greater empathy, respect, and awareness, fostering deeper connections and more effective communication, data collection, and interpretation within Black communities.

These are examples of the many Black ontologies. Life history researchers should always remember that the heterogeneity of Black communities implies that diverse Black ontologies and realities exist, and there is no one-size-fits-all approach to understanding them. How, then, do we understand them? This brings us to the concept of epistemology.

Epistemology is the study of knowledge. It addresses the relationship between the researcher (knower) and the reality being researched (the known). Going back to the obesity example, a question to ask would be how do we know that obesity is a health risk? Is it through counting how many people are living with obesity (collecting quantitative data) or analyzing first-person narratives and obesity expert accounts? The response to this question is rooted in one's understanding of obesity and how this knowledge can be discovered. Here is another example. Consider a research project that explores the experiences of Black women who migrated from the Caribbean to North America in the 1990s. Think about the nature of the reality that this project seeks—how do the experiences of these women exist? Imagine whether we collected numerical (quantitative) data that would tell us how many Black women currently living in the United States migrated in the 1990s. Would this be helpful data for answering our research question about these women's migration experiences? Of course not. Our ontological assumptions would be based on the fact that the reality we seek in such a project exists in the form of non-numerical (qualitative) data such as stories, narratives, or diary entries. Since we are looking for non-numerical data, we need strategies to understand such data. Such reality is subjective and multiple, as seen by the study participants. The nature of the type of data we seek (ontology) determines both how we would understand it (epistemology) and the methods we would use to collect it (methodology). By acknowledging and examining our ontological and epistemological assumptions, we can develop a more nuanced understanding of the research process and the knowledge we produce. Another important concept is axiology.

What Is Axiology?

Axiology is the branch of philosophy that studies values in research. It raises the question "Can research be neutral or do the personal values of the researcher shape how they design the study and implement it?" Axiology concerns the value system that guides the research process, including the researcher's worldview and their opinions about the research community and individual participants. The ubuntu ontology informs the axiological assumptions about researching Black people and people of African descent. As noted above, Ubuntu emphasizes interconnectedness, community, and mutual support. When applied to researching Black people and people of African descent, Ubuntu informs axiological assumptions or research values in several ways.

- *Interconnectedness and reciprocity:* Ubuntu emphasizes the importance of relationships and reciprocity. Researchers should approach participants with a sense of mutual respect, responsibility, and reciprocity, recognizing that knowledge is cocreated.
- *Community-centered approach:* Ubuntu prioritizes community over individualism. Researchers should value and involve communities in the research process, ensuring that the research is relevant, beneficial, and respectful.
- *Respect for elders and ancestors:* Ubuntu emphasizes the importance of respecting elders and ancestors. Researchers should acknowledge the historical and cultural contexts of the communities they study, showing respect for the knowledge and experiences of elders and ancestors.

- *Nonexploitative and equitable research practices:* Ubuntu promotes nonexploitative and equitable relationships. Researchers should ensure that their methods and practices are fair, transparent, and beneficial to the communities involved. According to Jean-Pierre et al. (2024, p. 5), researchers can enact Ubuntu "through an ethics of care toward community members." It is about ethics of care and cultural respect.

Axiology influences what researchers prioritize, how they interact with participants, and how they represent knowledge.

BOX 1.1   AXIOLOGY IN ACTION

Imagine you are an educated, independent scholar passionate about issues of social justice and anti-Black racism. You are conducting a life history research project with African American women who have experienced racial profiling and police brutality. One participant, Kemi, shares a story about her son's encounter with the police, which left him traumatized. What might your axiological stance involve?

1. **During the interview:**
   - Reflect on your social location and check in on any saviorism, supremacist, and racist tendencies. Remember that Black people and people of African descent are capable to navigate their own circumstances and do not require a savior. At the end of your research, you might step away from their community, but this remains their reality.
   - Value Kemi's experience, prioritize her narrative, acknowledge the pain and trauma she and her son have endured, and recognize the importance of centering such voices and experiences in research.

> – Know when to stop or pause to avoid causing any more harm or emotional distress.
>
> 2. **Data analysis and reporting:**
>
>   – Critically examine and challenge the dominant values and power structures that perpetuate systemic racism and police brutality. For example, in the discussion section of your paper, you can question the notion that the police are always justified in their actions.
>
>   – Do not disclose coping strategies without offering Kemi an opportunity to review them.

Axiology is important in life history research with Black people because it reminds researchers to be ethical, decolonial, and aligned with Black cultural values. It challenges exploitative research traditions, ensures that Black voices are respected, and protects against saviorism and supremacist research practices (Figure 1.1).

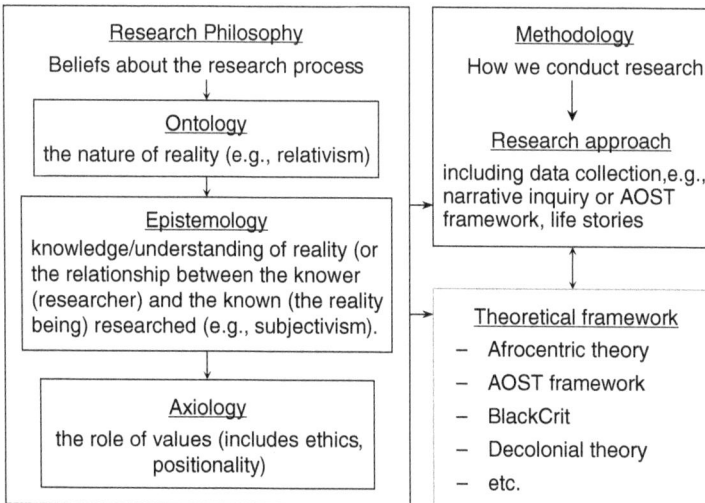

Figure 1.1   Relationship between philosophy, methodology, and theory

Source: Adapted from Jean-Pierre et al. (2024), Osei-Tutu (2023).

Axiological assumptions cover ethical considerations and positionality of the researcher. They play a critical role in ensuring that research is ethical and culturally appropriate.

Positionality

Positionality refers to the social, cultural, and personal background and values that shape a researcher's perspectives, experiences, and interactions with the research community (D'silva et al., 2016). For transparency and trustworthiness, researchers are usually expected to include a positionality statement in their works (Jean-Pierre & Collins, 2022). A positionality statement is a reflective statement to acknowledge and disclose their personal perspectives, biases, and social locations that may influence their research, analysis, and interpretation. It covers aspects of the researcher's social location relevant for the specific research project. These might include race, gender, sexuality, ability, and education status. Positionality plays a vital role in shaping the research process, particularly when working with Black communities. We should be careful not to use positionality statements in ways that establish and justify researcher authority and supremacy (King, 2024). King (2024, p. 6) writes that scholars "need to engage in this work more robustly and differently ... To be meaningful, positionality statements should engage with the aspects of the author's identity that are most relevant to the study and what these aspects of identity mean for the execution of the research."

It is important to note that the researcher's positionality facilitates the evolvement of shared understanding that are formed in their interactions with the participant(s), which results in the definition of the situation (Goffman, 1959). The shared definition of the situation involves interpreting cues such as body language, tone, setting, and allows the researcher and participant to coordinate their actions and act appropriately. The researcher's positionality should therefore be a proactive and ongoing process, rather than a one-time consideration.

Positionality Statement Examples

Example 1: Akuoko-Barfi et al. (2025) studied Black youth navigating policing in Ontario, Canada. Drawing on Jacobson and Mustafa's (2019) application of positioning one's identity in research, the authors of this paper recognized that their experiences informed how they interpreted their data. All five authors are racialized, two are Black, and one identifies as a member of the Caribbean diaspora. From their own lived experiences, the researchers came to understand and analyze how ethno-racial identity can intrude on one's ability to successfully navigate—or remain imperceptible to—public systems (Akuoko-Barfi et al., 2025, p. 111).

Example 2: Ramdeo (2025), citing others (Beoku-Betts, 1994; Collins, 1986; Egharevba, 2001; Few et al., 2003; Nelson, 1996; Vass, 2017), utilized narrative inquiry to study UK Black women educators' experiences of hindered careers and workplace psychological harm in school environments. They write as follows:

Researcher positionality plays a central role in the willingness of marginalised groups and individuals to openly provide sensitive and personal information through the research process. As a racialised female researcher (and former schoolteacher) but not race-matched (Egharevba, 2001; Vass, 2017) to the four Black women educators, I cannot claim to know what it is like to be a Black woman, but the echoes of similarity in our experiences allowed me to stand in solidarity with them and want to expose their oppressions to drive for change. Self-reflexivity heightened my consciousness of my insider and outsider status and the researcher/researched power relations during the interview process and through to analysis and reporting. I acknowledge that phenotypically I look South Asian but with the hybridity of my ethnicity, cultural background and history being Indo-Caribbean, I assumed I would be granted access to Black women educators' lives due to cultural commonalities with some participants. This was not necessarily the case. Presumption of insider status based on certain shared identities is not sufficient. Few et al. (2003) cite Nelson (1996) to draw on the concept of "gradations of endogeny" (2003, p. 207), described as being the emotional and psychological subjectivity that research participants use to determine the extent of legitimate researcher insiderness acting as an internal gatekeeper to the level of access a researcher can gain to their research participants. Therefore, as a method of trust building, I shared my ethnic, cultural and employment background with participants, to circumvent scepticism and discover commonalities, in a hope to become an insider by negotiation (Beoku-Betts, 1994). However, I was acutely aware that I was racially an outsider to these Black women's experiences, despite employment experiences placing me nearer an insider to their own racialised employment experiences. Self-reflexivity enabled me to recognise that I sit somewhere in between, or an outsider-within (Collins, 1986), as a conduit to provide a platform for these women's voices, thoughts and ideas.

In researching Black women, it was important to reflect on and address specific nuances that may cause potential harm to enable trust and respect of the participants. (Ramdeo, 2025, pp. 481–482)

When conducting life history research with Black communities, positionality, instead of just a retrospective exercise, should be a forward-looking, solidarity-driven practice that enhances ethical and socially responsible scholarship (Gani & Khan, 2024; Zembylas, 2025). While we can always advocate for studying marginalized communities from the insider's perspective instead of an outsider's or the emic and etic view (Pike, 1967), it is important to note that when it comes to conducting life history research with Black communities, one can never fully be an insider unless they have the embodied experience of being Black. Having insiderness refers to having automatic acceptance in the community. The diversity of Black and people of African descent means that simply being Black does not automatically grant acceptance within all Black communities. In North America, for example, Black communities are multifaceted, shaped by differences in country of origin, ethnicity, language, education, socioeconomic status, gender and sexual identity, age, family status, location, ability, etc. Nonetheless, researchers can engage as allies. Researching from the vantage point of an ally demands a commitment from the researcher to do the work to grow and approach the community with cultural sensitivity, humility, and empathy while acknowledging that the level of insiderness is limited.

Although the positionality statements by Akuoko-Barfi et al. (2025) and Ramdeo (2025) are good examples, acknowledging positionality should not be a fixed but a dynamic process that varies across different social, cultural, historical, and geographical contexts. It is crucial to think through our positionality and question our intentions and their potential harmful consequences for the researched and for the research at the outset. For example, as a researcher with your current social location, what is your worldview about the specific Black community you are studying, and what ontological and axiological beliefs do you hope to bring to the individual participants, the community, and your readers? Researchers should not leave their readers with questions about their social location and its relevance to Black communities. Utilize positionality statements as a transformative tool to embed ethical research practices, moving beyond mere methodological compliance.

Epistemological and Ontological Positions

Now you have some basic understanding of ontological, epistemological, and axiological assumptions. Let us turn to the ontological and epistemological approaches to conducting life history research with Black people, emphasizing the need for culturally responsive and decolonial approaches. Recent scholarship has highlighted the importance of centering Black perspectives, knowledge, and ways of knowing in research (Best, 2022; Hines, 2024; Osei-Tutu, 2021a; Starks, 2022). There are two main interrelated approaches: constructivism and interpretivism.

Life history research is rooted in a **constructivist** paradigm, which posits that reality is socially constructed and subjective. This perspective acknowledges that *individuals' experiences are shaped by their unique contexts, cultures, and histories.* Life history researchers embrace this ontological stance, recognizing that participants' narratives are not objective truths but rather co-constructed accounts of their experiences (Kingsman & Davis, 2024). Life history research is also rooted in the **interpretivist** paradigm, or the belief that *there are multiple realities relative to an individual's set of experiences, beliefs, and understandings.* Hence, reality is relative. In interpretivism, there is no absolute truth, and this ontology is called **relativism.** Life history research with Black communities can therefore be **constructed** (e.g., by the researcher and the participant) or **interpreted** though a meaning-making process engaged in by the researcher.

Engaging in life history research with Black communities therefore implies that as a researcher you will be involved in co-constructing and interpreting knowledge. It is thus important to recognize the historical and ongoing injustices against Black communities. Black people's life experiences are shaped by intersecting forms of oppression, including racism, sexism, homophobia, and classism (Crenshaw, 1998; McClish, 2018; McClish-Boyd & Bhattacharya, 2024). Epistemologically, life history research is grounded in the **interpretivist** tradition, which emphasizes the importance of **subjective** experience and meaning making. As researchers, we cannot avoid influencing the way our participants act and behave and vice versa. Together, we co-construct reality. Reality is therefore not stable but subjective. This epistemological stance is called **subjectivism** (Table 1.1).

Table 1.1 Philosophical Assumptions for Conducting Life History Research With Black people

Type of assumption	Constructivism	Interpretivism	Implications for research with Black communities
Ontology (nature of reality): Relativism	Reality is shaped through social interaction and individuals' interpretations of multiple realities. Example: A person's understanding of obesity may vary based on their ethnicity, culture, geographical location, life experiences, etc.	Reality is not fixed but relative. There are multiple realities. Example: The meaning of "a family" may vary across societies, cultures, spatial locations, and time.[2]	Recognize diverse voices of members of Black communities. There is no single universal Black experience. Researchers should consider different participants' perspectives.

(Continued)

---

[2]For example, Canada's family landscape is diverse and ever evolving. Traditional nuclear families, comprising a married couple with children, are just one of many family structures. Blended families, where stepparents and stepsiblings join together, are becoming increasingly common. Single-parent families are also prevalent. Families with same-sex parents are gaining visibility. Extended family arrangements where grandparents or other relatives play a caregiving role are significant as well. Additionally, some people choose nontraditional living arrangements, such as multigenerational households. This variety reflects Canada's cultural mosaic, with people from numerous ethnic and cultural backgrounds bringing their unique traditions and values to family life. Overall, Canadian families are complex, dynamic, and multifaceted, reflecting the country's rich social fabric.

Table 1.1   (Continued)

Type of assumption	Constructivism	Interpretivism	Implications for research with Black communities
Epistemology (nature of knowledge): Subjectivism	The researcher and participant co-construct knowledge in the "field" Example: In life history research, the researcher and the participant influence each other's actions and behaviors.	Knowledge is gained through interpretations, not objective observations. Example: A researcher studying teacher–student relationships would explore how teachers and students interpret their roles instead of aiming to uncover one reality.	The relationship between the researcher and participant should be borne in mind throughout the study process. Center Black narratives in the analysis rather than perspectives imposed by dominant groups.
Methodology How to conduct research	Researchers focus on how individuals construct meaning in specific contexts.	Researchers interpret social meanings based on participants' lived experiences.	Avoid Euro-Western frameworks that ignore structural racism and historical oppression.

Source: Based on the ideas of Best (2022), Hines (2024), McGibbon and Etowa (2009), Osei-Tutu (2021a), and Starks (2022).

As a researcher, you must keep such assumptions at the back of your mind in the process of collecting, analyzing, and disseminating data. In conclusion, life history research is rooted in a complex web of ontological and epistemological assumptions. Constructivist and interpretivist perspectives underpin this approach. As life history research continues to evolve, it is essential that Black and Africana studies scholars continually engage with these debates and developments to ensure that these methodologies remain a robust and nuanced tool for understanding human experience.

THEORETICAL FRAMEWORKS

Conducting research with Black people and people of African descent requires a thoughtful and intentional approach, one that acknowledges the historical and ongoing impacts of systemic racism, colonization, and oppression. By using some traditional research paradigms, one risks perpetuating these injustices, prioritizing dominant epistemologies and methodologies that erase or marginalize Black voices and experiences. For those who want to ensure that their research is grounded in theoretical frameworks that center Black perspectives, epistemologies, and ontologies, in this chapter, I offer several options of theoretical frameworks for consideration.

African Oral Traditional Storytelling Framework (AOTS Framework)

The African oral traditional storytelling framework (AOTS framework; Osei-Tutu, 2021a) offers a culturally nuanced, ethically informed, and philosophically grounded approach to understanding the diverse experiences of Black people (Osei-Tutu, 2021a, 2023). It was developed in a study of African immigrant families' experiences of retaining and transmitting their cultural identity and languages while navigating a racialized educational system in the United States (Osei-Tutu, 2021a). In his work, Osei-Tutu (2021a, 2023) disrupts the traditional researcher–participant dynamic and adopts a more collaborative and equitable approach. He contends that

> research in the AOTS Framework is with a communal learning and knowing together approach, where collaborators are part "owners" in the study. They are not "participating" in their own lived experiences (that is, collaborators are not taking part in a study about their lives); they are privileging the researcher by sharing their knowledges and experiences with them. (Osei-Tutu, 2021b, p. 3)

In the AOTS framework, the concept of story gathering replaces the conventional data collection in recognition that people's lived experiences cannot be collected like objects. Instead, the AOTS framework honors the fact that the researcher has the privilege of sharing and weaving together individual narratives, which is made possible by centering the framework within the communal cultural contexts of Black communities (Osei-Tutu, 2021b).

Key Tenets of the AOTS Framework

- *Communal knowledge sharing:* Knowledge is shared, not owned. Research is a collaborative process where participants are cocreators of knowledge rather than passive subjects.
- *Storytelling as a research method:* Stories are not just data but vehicles for cultural knowledge, resistance, and meaning making. Storytelling traditions among Black people and people of African descent include songs, proverbs, ceremonies, ideophones, and metaphorical language.
- *Decolonization and anti-racist pedagogy:* The AOTS framework challenges Western epistemologies that marginalize minority perspectives. It centers Black people's worldviews in research, resisting colonial and racist narratives.
- *Linguistic and cultural authenticity:* Research should prioritize participants' languages, symbols, and storytelling methods to maintain authenticity. Black people and people of African descent have proverbs and idioms that preserve cultural depth and meaning and should be analyzed in research.
- *Sankofa principle ("go back and get it"):* A guiding philosophy meaning learning from the past to build the future encourages Africana studies researchers to return to their traditions for knowledge production.

Steps to Apply the AOTS Framework in Research

The framework is applied through two key processes:

Story gathering is done in a "by the fireside" or fireside space, which is a community gathering involving a group of people with or without food and drinks (Osei-Tutu, 2021b). The fireside has three attributes: It is communal and is characterized by public education and storytelling. Unlike Western research methods that extract data, story gathering fosters mutual learning between researcher and participants/collaborators. Researchers can initiate conversations with their own stories, encouraging participants to share theirs naturally.

Co-telling and co-making meaning. The AOTS framework is a process in which research collaborators (participants) are actively involved in shaping how their stories are interpreted. Stories are generated/told, reviewed, and revised collaboratively to ensure authentic representation. The discussions in the fireside space emphasize Black perspectives, historical contexts, and lived realities.

The AOTS framework is a powerful framework for studying Black people and people of African descent. It empowers Black communities by valuing their cultural identities and knowledge systems. It can be utilized as a methodology as well as an analytical tool.

Afrocentric Theory

Afrocentric theory, or Afrocentricity, is a framework in which phenomena are viewed from the perspective of the African person (Asante, 1991, 2020). Founded by Asante, Afrocentricity is the opposite of Eurocentrism. It underscores placing African experiences and perspectives at the center of analyses concerning people of African descent. It seeks to counter Eurocentric narratives by validating African cultural expressions, histories, and philosophies. Afrocentric theory emphasizes spirituality, the interconnectedness of all beings, the centrality of collective identity and responsibility, and the significance of lived experiences. Research informed by Afrocentric theory should advocate for the agency of Black people in developing solutions to political, social, and economic challenges, challenging oppressive structures by restoring and valuing historically marginalized Black knowledge (Jean-Pierre et al., 2024). Afrocentricity scholars argue that the dislocation of Africans from their own cultural perspectives is a form of intellectual and cultural terrorism that erodes their sense of self. Asante (2020) challenges the hierarchy of cultural dominance, particularly the projection of European superiority over African cultures.

Although Afrocentricity was originally developed as a framework for understanding the cultural identity of Black people on the African continent, it remains highly relevant for life history research with Black diasporic communities. It is a relevant framework for ensuring that Black people and people of African descent control how their stories are documented by decentering Eurocentric perspectives. For example, life history researchers should ensure that the values, beliefs, customs, traditions, languages, customs, spirituality, kinship, and rituals of Black people are ethically collected, documented, and reported in ways that decenter Eurocentric epistemologies and ontologies.

Applying Afrocentricity to the study of Black people requires a framework that centers African cultural values, perspectives, and agency in research (Table 1.2).

Table 1.2   Guide to Practical Application of Afrocentricity

Points to consider	Practical application
Ground yourself in Afrocentricity.	Understand Afrocentricity as a paradigm that positions Afro-descendant people as subjects, not objects, of study.
Define research questions.	Critically review literature that speaks to your topic from an Afrocentric perspective.
	Formulate questions that reflect African worldviews, historical contexts, and cultural knowledge.
	Ensure that research seeks to uplift, empower, and accurately represent Black stories and communities rather than reinforce Western biases.

Points to consider	Practical application
Use culturally relevant methodologies.	Incorporate Black-centered epistemologies that emphasize individual as well as collective wisdom, spirituality, and identity. Use data collection methods that align with Back people's traditions such as oral histories and storytelling.
	Replace deficit-based frameworks with agency-driven, strengths-based perspectives.
Interpret findings through an African-centered lens.	Situate findings within the rich cultural heritage and diverse traditions of Black and Afro-descendant communities, acknowledging their historical depth and continuity.
	Highlight the resilience, agency, creativity, and contributions of Black people and people of African descent to global civilization and the global economy.
Promote ethical research practices.	Acknowledge and respect the philosophical and ethical systems of Afro-descendant people.
	Ensure that research is not exploitative but prioritizes mutual benefit and respect.
	Continuously reflect on your positionality as you speak, listen, record data, and interpret it.

Source: Adapted from Asante (2020).

Applying Afrocentricity to the study of Black people requires a framework that centers African cultural values, perspectives, and agency in research.

Black Feminist Thought

Black feminist thought (BFT) is a theoretical framework that emerged in the 1970s and 1980s, primarily in the United States (Collins, 2009). It is a critical theory that analyzes the intersectionality of race, gender, class, sexuality, age, and other categories of difference that Black women face (Collins, 2009; McClish, 2018). BFT therefore provides a nuanced understanding of Black women's experiences and challenges their systematic exclusion from dominant US cultural narratives (Collins, 2009). It postulates that dominant narratives tokenize Black communities in research and literature and advocates for culturally relevant and justice-oriented approaches. BFT is especially valuable in studies on systemic inequalities, trauma, identity, and empowerment.

The core tenets of BFT include the following:

- *Intersectionality:* BFT recognizes that Black women's experiences are shaped by multiple intersecting forms of oppression, including racism, sexism, lesbophobia, transphobia misogyny, and classism.
- *Centering Black women's voices:* BFT prioritizes the voices, experiences, and perspectives of Black women, who have historically been marginalized and excluded from dominant feminist and anti-racist movements.
- *Critique of white feminism:* BFT critiques the limitations and biases of white feminism, which has often ignored or erased the experiences of Black women.
- *Emphasis on empowerment:* BFT seeks to empower Black women and promote their self-determination, autonomy, and agency.

Postcolonial Theory

Postcolonial theory was developed during the mid- to late 20th century. Notable proponents include Edward Said, Homi Bhabha, and Gayatri Spivak. Other notable scholars include Frantz Fanon, Albert Memmi, and Ngugi wa Thiong'o. The conversation on postcolonial theory can be better understood when it begins with the topics of colonialism and colonization. The project of colonialism silenced the languages, cultures, religions, and political and economic spheres of the colonized. Everything of the colonizer was placed at the center, whereas those of the colonized were either silenced or placed at the periphery (Memmi, 2013). Thus, postcolonialism is usually concerned with "a politics of opposition and struggle" against the remaining effects of colonialism (Mishra & Hodge, 1991, p. 399) By realizing that the colonized has historically always been pushed to the periphery, postcolonialism seeks to "problematize the key [contemporary] relationship between centre and periphery" (p. 276). As Young (2020a) asserts, postcolonialism brings together various perspectives and disciplines, including issues related to feminism, social justice, and ecology. The core mission of postcolonialism is to "change the way people think, the way they behave, to produce a more just and equitable relation between the different peoples of the world" (p. 7). The postcolonial framework makes a critical call to decolonize knowledge production through challenging Western dominance in knowledge production and diversifying data sources.

Below are the two key tenets of postcolonial theory that I wish to highlight.

Challenge Western Dominance in Knowledge Creation

The foundation for postcolonial theory was laid by Edward Said (1978), who critiqued Western representations of non-Western cultures, arguing that they perpetuated negative stereotypes (e.g., weak, backward, irrational). Said identified binary oppositions (e.g., Orient vs. Occident, Europeans vs. Others, East vs. West, Us vs. Them). Such binary positions feminized non-Western cultures, associating them with irrationality and lack of capacity for democracy, and masculinized the West, who were portrayed as civilized, rational, and democratic (Said, 1978). To respectfully conduct research with Black people and people of African descent, researchers should intentionally recognize and challenge these binaries, seeking alternative representations to promote a more nuanced understanding of non-Western cultures.

Recognize Cultural Hybridity and Diversify Data Sources

Building on the work of Said (1978), Bhabha (1984, 1994) introduced the concept of hybridity. He suggested that the cultural exchange between Western and non-Western creates "the mixedness, or even impurity of cultures" (Huddart, 2006, p. 4). Bhabha advocates for a postcolonial analysis that focuses on the "borderlines" of cultures. However, Bhabha's tenet of hybridity downplays the cultural harm inflicted on Black people and people of African descent. Additionally, hybridity ignores other sociopolitical factors that define epistemic injustices against Black communities. Using critical hybridity, which is combining a variety of methodologies and seeking out different types of knowledge, as well as contextual dialogues could minimize the weaknesses of the hybridity perspective (Forsyth et al., 2017). Hence, researchers who study Black communities in the diaspora should consider using a nuanced approach to postcolonial analysis that recognizes and acknowledges the intricate, hybrid nature of their cultural identities and diversify knowledge sources. For example, apart from oral stories, researchers could seek visual representations such as photographs and cultural objects/artifacts.

Critical Race Theory

Critical Race Theory (CRT) is a theoretical framework that examines how race and racism intersect with power and privilege in society. CRT critiques the idea of a colorblind, meritocratic society, arguing that racism is embedded in institutions, laws, and social norms, perpetuating inequality and oppression. CRT emerged in the 1970s and 1980s, primarily in the United States, as a response to the limitations of traditional civil rights approaches. It draws on various disciplines, including sociology, law, education, and cultural studies. It is argued that people who have not grasped the tenets of CRT often misrepresent it (Ladson-Billings, 2021). According to Ladson-Billings (2021), CRT is not merely about discussing race or racial issues; it is a theoretical framework that construes racism as a standard and ingrained aspect of American society.

Key Tenets of CRT

Ladson-Billings (2021) outlines the key tenets of CRT as follows:

- *Interest convergence:* Marginalized groups, particularly racial minorities, only achieve racial justice when their interests align with those of the dominant group. In other words, progress is made when it benefits or does not harm the dominant group.

- *Race as a social construction:* CRT argues that race is not a biological fact but rather a social construct created to justify discrimination, oppression, and inequality. This means that racial categories are not fixed or natural but instead are fluid and subject to change based on social, economic, and political contexts.

- *Intersectionality:* This tenet recognizes that individuals have multiple identities (e.g., race, class, gender, sexuality, disability) that intersect and interact to produce unique experiences of discrimination and oppression. Intersectionality highlights the need to consider these multiple identities when analyzing social issues.

- *Counter-narratives:* CRT challenges dominant narratives and amplifies counter-narratives that highlight the experiences of marginalized groups.

- *Racism is systemic:* Racism is not just individual prejudice but is embedded in institutions, laws, and social norms.

- *Power and privilege:* CRT examines how power and privilege are distributed and maintained, often to the detriment of marginalized groups.

- *Social justice:* CRT aims to dismantle systems of oppression and promote social justice and equity.

According to Jean-Pierre et al. (2024), it is important to avoid categorizing Black people within broad groups, such as visible minorities or racialized populations, without adequately addressing the specific deprivations associated with being Black, which results in a partial analysis. Conducting life history research should focus on Blackness in relation to the study topic. Examples of studies that have used life history method focusing on Blackness include Lykes (1983) and Sosulski et al. (2010).

CRT is a practical framework for understanding racial inequalities, especially in the contexts of Black people and people of

African descent. It lays the foundation for other theories and frameworks, including Black feminist thought (discussed above), critical Black theory (BlackCrit), and intersectionality.

Critical Black Theory

Critical Black theory (BlackCrit) is an extension of CRT made popular by Dumas and Ross (2016). BlackCrit specifically centers anti-Blackness as a fundamental organizing principle of social life (Wallace, 2022). According to Wallace (2022), unlike CRT, which examines race broadly in relation to white supremacy, BlackCrit insists that Blackness is taken to be not merely another racial category but a distinct ontological position that is structurally opposed to humanity. It critiques pathologized conceptions of identity, institutional racism, and the normalization of white supremacist structures presented as neutral. BlackCrit has gained popularity in Black studies as a theory for analyzing experiences and representations of Black people (Jean-Pierre et al., 2024; Reed, 2022; Wallace, 2022).

According to Wallace (2022) there are four foundational pillars of BlackCrit:

- *Anti-Blackness as justification for violence and harm*: BlackCrit posits that anti-Blackness (the opposition between Blackness and humanity) is a foundational aspect of society, rendering Blackness as inherently nonhuman. Anti-Blackness is a justification to inflict violence against Black people and also recruits non-Black people of color, pitting them against Blackness.
- *The legacy of slavery*: BlackCrit asserts that the legacy of slavery continues to shape Black existence, positioning Black people as property/objects rather than human beings.
- *Black-centered versus people-of-color-centered frameworks*: The BlackCrit framework critiques broad racial categories like "people of color" for failing to recognize "(anti)blackness

as the organizing principle of social life" (Wallace, 2022, p. 379). Frameworks that subsume blackness under people of color are not only inherently anti-Blackist but also distort the uniqueness of Blackness vis-à-vis people of color. This results in a flawed understanding of anti-Blackness, overlooking its unique characteristics.

- *Point of departure from CRT*: According to Wallace, unlike CRT, which centers white supremacy as the dominant racial logic, BlackCrit focuses on anti-Blackness as a distinct structural phenomenon. While CRT assumes that racial progress is possible through policy and legal reform, BlackCrit is more skeptical about reform within existing structures. CRT emphasizes racism as a systemic problem affecting all people of color, while BlackCrit argues that Blackness is uniquely positioned outside of the realm of the human. The unique tenets of BlackCrit make it more applicable to life history research with Black people and people of African descent.

BlackCrit theorists believe that by conducting comprehensive analyses that carefully examine the complex experiences of Black people and people of African descent, researchers can help counteract harmful and inaccurate narratives about these groups often present in scholarly research and literature. BlackCrit theorists take a positive view of the future of blackness, unlike Afropessimists (proponents of Afropessimism), who do not see any possibility for change. Afropessimism is a critical philosophical and theoretical framework that argues that anti-Blackness is a fundamental and structural feature of the world, particularly in the context of Western modernity (Wekker, 2021). Similar to BlackCrit, Afropessimism argues that gratuitous violence against Black people is a unique and distinct form of violence that cannot be compared to the experiences of other, non-Black groups. This perspective also theorizes slavery as a foundational social relation that defines Blackness as fundamentally opposed to humanity (Terrefe, 2020). Afropessimists believe that anti-Blackness is structural and resistant to change. Despite its pessimistic ideas, Afropessimism has been influential in a range of fields, including Black studies, critical theory, and cultural studies and has been used to analyze a wide range of topics, from racism and police violence to education and cultural representation.

Intersectionality

Intersectionality is a term that was coined by Black feminist scholar Kimberlé Crenshaw in 1989. A critical framework, intersectionality posits that individuals possess multiple identities (e.g., race, class, gender, sexuality, disability) that intersect and interact to produce unique experiences of discrimination and marginalization (Crenshaw, 1989, 1991). It highlights how marginalized people face overlapping systems of discrimination rather than single-axis oppression. For example, Black women experience racism and sexism simultaneously in ways that differ from Black men or white women. Intersectionality is widely used in social justice, law, and research to address systemic inequalities. It challenges one-size-fits-all approaches and promotes inclusive policies that recognize diverse lived experiences within marginalized communities. Intersectionality is an analytical tool that is sometimes perceived as a method as well as a disposition (Runyan, 2018). Black people and people of African descent in the diaspora face compounded marginalization by being located at the intersection of being dark-skinned and the offspring of enslaved people (McClish-Boyd & Bhattacharya, 2024). Crenshaw critiques the single-axis framework and argues for demarginalization of the intersection of race and sex.

Key Tenets of Intersectionality

- *Multiple identities*: Intersectionality recognizes that individuals have multiple identities that cannot be reduced to a single category. People hold multiple identities that influence their life trajectories.

- *Overlapping systems of oppression and privilege*: People's multiple identities intersect to produce unique experiences of oppression and privilege that cannot be understood by examining a single form of oppression (e.g., racism, ableism, sexism) in isolation. For example, a low-income LGBTQ immigrant may face multiple barriers beyond just race or class.
- *Power dynamics*: Intersectionality emphasizes the role of power dynamics in shaping experiences of oppression, highlighting how dominant groups maintain power over marginalized groups.
- *Contextualizing experiences*: Intersectionality stresses the importance of contextualizing individual experiences within specific social, historical, and cultural contexts. For example, a Black woman in 1970s faced different challenges than one in 2025 in the United States.
- *Lived experiences are central to understanding oppression and privilege.* Therefore, first-person narratives are crucial for a meaningful evidence-based change. For example, collecting first-person narratives is better than analyzing media content.

The Usefulness of Intersectionality for Studying Black Communities

- Intersectionality recognizes that Black people in the diaspora often face multiple forms of oppression, including racism, xenophobia, classism, sexism, police brutality, and mass incarceration.
- Intersectionality highlights the complexity of Black identity. It acknowledges that Black identity is complex and multifaceted, encompassing various ethnicities, nationalities, cultures, and experiences.
- Intersectionality offers a framework for analyzing how power dynamics shape the experiences of Black individuals and communities in the diaspora.

- Intersectionality emphasizes the importance of contextual-izing analysis within specific social, historical, and cultural contexts, which is essential for understanding the diverse experiences of Black communities in the diaspora.
- Intersectionality is a powerful framework for understanding the complex experiences of Black communities in the diaspora.

While intersectionality is not without its limitations and criti-cisms, it remains a crucial tool for scholars, activists, and policymakers seeking to address the complex social justice issues facing Black communities in the diaspora. To add value to life history research with Black communities, intersectionality can be applied to the analysis of the heterogenous aspects of Black experiences and identity.

Decolonial Theory

Decolonial theory builds on anti-colonialism, which initially referred to physical struggles against colonial empires. However, anti-colonialism has evolved to encompass movements, thoughts, and practices that resist colonial domination and imperialism. Decolonial theory recognizes that even after colonial empires withdrew (from Africa for example), colonial structures, dis-courses, and relations persisted (Go, 2023; Sajed & Seidel, 2023). Decolonial theory seeks to challenge and change these systemic structures, particularly in academia and research (Noxolo, 2017). Noxolo (2017) illustrates that decolonial the-ory arises from the experiences and struggles of Indigenous peoples who continue to face the impacts of colonization. It advocates for "delinking from the historical and ongoing ine-qualities rooted in European imperialism" (p. 342). In other words, decolonial theory advocates for recognizing Indigenous agency and knowledge. It aims to challenge and eventually change the global practices rooted in the colonial mindset that are evident in Western academic spaces in both Western and non-Western contexts (McArthur, 2022). According to McArthur (2022), decolonial scholarship should bring "transformative change" (p. 1690) by provoking deliberate efforts to go beyond the rhetoric of decolonization to embrace Indigenous perspectives while addressing historical power imbalances. This also includes recognizing multiple histories and epistemologies while drawing on colonial experiences (Mignolo, 2007).

Applying Decolonial Theory to Research with Black People and People of African Descent

Decolonial theory offers a critical framework for researchers to challenge dominant Western epistemologies and center the experiences and knowledge of marginalized communities, particularly Black and people of African descent. As researchers, it is essential to acknowledge the historical power dynamics that have shaped the production of knowledge about Black communities.

First, researchers must recognize and acknowledge the ways in which Western knowledge systems have been imposed on Black people of African descent, erasing their Indigenous knowledge systems and cultural practices (Mignolo, 2007). Researchers must be willing to decenter Western knowledge and instead center Black and Africana epistemologies, such as Afrocentricity, which prioritizes African cultural and historical experiences (Asante, 2018).

Second, researchers must adopt a decolonial methodology that prioritizes reciprocity, mutual respect, and the cocreation of knowledge. This involves building trust with Black communities and recognizing their agency and expertise. Researchers must be willing to listen to and learn from the participants in research rather than imposing their own assumptions and frameworks (Smith, 2012). This requires a willingness to be vulnerable, to acknowledge one's own limitations and biases, and to be open to feedback and critique. Researchers must be aware of their own positionality and how it shapes their research questions, methods, and findings (Crenshaw, 1998). This demands a commitment to reflexivity, transparency, and accountability throughout the research process.

Finally, researchers must prioritize the well-being and safety of Black research participants. This involves recognizing the potential risks and harms associated with research, particularly for marginalized communities. Researchers must take steps to minimize these risks, such as obtaining informed consent, ensuring confidentiality and anonymity, and providing support and resources for participants.

In conclusion, applying decolonial theory to life history research with Black diasporic people requires a fundamental shift in how we approach knowledge production and mobilization. It involves recognizing and challenging dominant Western epistemologies, adopting a decolonial methodology, being mindful of power dynamics, and prioritizing the well-being and safety of participants. By doing so, researchers can cocreate knowledge that is grounded in the perspectives and experiences of Black people and people of African descent.

The theoretical frameworks described above and summarized in Table 1.3 are examples of the many frameworks that can be utilized in researching with Black people and people of African descent.

Table 1.3 Summary of Theoretical Frameworks

Framework	Description	Examples of relevant disciplines
AOTS	A collaborative and equitable approach in which researchers and "collaborators" (research participants) cocreate knowledge.	Black studies, Africana studies, African studies and related fields
Afrocentricity	A framework that centers African perspectives and experiences, countering Eurocentric narratives by validating Black cultural expressions, histories, and philosophies.	Black studies, Africana studies, African studies, and related fields

Framework	Description	Examples of relevant disciplines
Black feminist thought	Focuses on the intersections between racism, sexism, and other forms of oppression. This theory highlights the importance of centering Black women's experiences and perspectives.	Black studies, Africana studies, African studies, and related fields
Postcolonial theory	Explores the legacies of colonialism and imperialism on Black people's lives. This framework can help analyze how historical and ongoing colonialism influences Black people's life histories.	General social sciences and humanities
Critical race theory (CRT)	Examines how race and racism intersect with power and inequality in society. CRT can help analyze the ways in which systemic racism shapes Black people's life histories.	General social sciences and humanities
Black critical theory (BlackCrit)	Centers anti-Blackness as a fundamental organizing principle of social life. BlackCrit posits that Blackness is not merely another racial category but a distinct ontological position.	Black studies, Africana studies, African studies, and related fields
Intersectionality	Examines how multiple forms of oppression and privilege intersect to shape individual experiences.	General social sciences and humanities
Decolonial theory	Seeks to challenge and dismantle the dominant Western epistemologies and power structures that characterize conventional research methodologies.	General social sciences and humanities

Source: Compiled from the ideas of Asante (1991, 2020), Bhabha (1984, 1994), Collins (2009), Crenshaw (1989, 1991), Dumas and Ross (2016), Ladson-Billings (2021), Noxolo (2017), Osei-Tutu (2021a, 2023), and Said (1978).

Integrating such frameworks and tools in life history research with Black communities will be helpful if you seek to decolonize knowledge production, challenge dominant narratives, and amplify the voices and experiences of Black people and people of African descent. I suggest that you aim for an approach or framework that acknowledges the historical trauma and ongoing struggles Black communities face, while also honoring their resilience, creativity, and agency. Centering Black perspectives and epistemologies in research is important for producing a more nuanced understanding of the complex experiences of Black people.

SUMMARY

This chapter introduced specific strategies for conducting life history research with Black people and people of African descent. This is a community that has experienced persistent social and epistemic injustices, necessitating thoughtful and nuanced approaches to address these complex issues. The current injustices, including anti-Blackness and racism, are deeply rooted in the history of enslavement and colonization, and life history researchers should engage in scholarship that challenges and disrupts rather than perpetuates them. This chapter has highlighted the importance of recognizing Black ontologies, such as Sankofa, Ubuntu, and Nommo, which embody distinct forms of Black wisdom. I have argued that researchers studying life histories should approach their work with a deep understanding and consideration of these ontologies. A wide variety of theoretical frameworks can be applied to life history research with Black people and people of African descent. The examples I give in this book include the AOTS Framework (Osei-Tutu, 2021a), Afrocentric theory, or Afrocentricity (Asante, 1991, 2020), postcolonial theory, critical race theory, and intersectionality. Black-focused frameworks that center Blackness and disrupt anti-Blackness can yield a more nuanced understanding of the complex experiences of Black people and people of African descent.

FURTHER READINGS

Anderson, E. (2022). *Black in white space: The enduring impact of color in everyday life.* The University of Chicago Press.

Asante, M. (1998). *The Afrocentric idea* (rev. ed.). Temple University Press.

Asante, M. K. (2020). Afrocentricity. In R. Rabaka (Ed.), *The Routledge handbook of pan-Africanism* (pp. 147–158). Routledge. https://doi.org/10.4324/9780429020193

Asante, M. K., Baldwin, J. A., Butler, J. E., Cain, R. A., Chimezie, A., Clarke, J. H., Davis, R. A., Aldridge, D. P., & James, E. L. (2021). *Africana studies: Philosophical perspectives and theoretical paradigms.* Washington State University Press. https://doi.org/10.4324/9781315433370

Collins, P. H. (2009). *Black feminist thought.* Routledge.

Diverlus, R., Hudson, S., & Ware, S. M. (Eds.). (2020). *Until we are free: Reflections on Black lives matter in Canada.* University of Regina Press. https://doi.org/10.1515/9780889776968

Maynard, R. (2017). *Policing Black lives: State violence in Canada from slavery to the present.* Fernwood Publishing.

McDougal, S., III. (2017). *Research methods in Africana studies* (rev. ed.). Peter Lang. International Academic Publishers.

Nayar, J. (2022). Returning the anti-colonial to philosophy. In *Beyond law and development* (pp. 58–79). Routledge.

Nayar, J. (2024). *Being anti-colonial.* Daraja Press.

Tamale, S. (2020). *Decolonization and Afro-feminism.* Daraja Press.

CHAPTER 2
Life History Research Design

At the design stage of a research project with Black populations, it is important to be aware of the existence of multiple Black ontologies, different worldviews and conceptions of what constitutes existence and reality among Afro-descendant peoples. To understand Black ontologies, researchers should acknowledge that s' realities are shaped by fluctuating and diverse notions of time, space, place and transcendence.

(Jean-Pierre et al., 2024, p. 4)

Life history research with Black and African diasporic communities requires flexibility and adaptability. Given the diverse cultures and values within each community, research designs must be tailored to reflect the distinct characteristics of the community being studied. A life history researcher usually goes to the field with an open mind and assumptions about the community of interest (Goodson & Sikes, 2016). The first steps in designing a life history research project would be identifying the research problem and formulating the research question. Designing a life history research project requires making a good plan rooted in your ontological and epistemological assumptions while aligning with your research question as well as participants' cultural protocols. In this chapter, you will learn about how to formulate a research problem, research question, and recruit participants.

RESEARCH PROBLEM

A research problem is a particular issue that requires investigation (Creswell & Poth, 2024). Identifying a research problem in life history research starts with *defining the research topic or selecting a broad area of interest.* Here are some examples of broad research topics:

- Black people's postmigration experiences in New York
- Spirituality and mental health among Black communities in Finland
- Education and social mobility among Black communities in Quebec, Canada.

This will be your working topic. Remember that as you move through the process, your research topic can change or be modified or revised to fit the literature as you formulate the research question. A common mistake many students make is to start with a topic and try to fit everything in this topic. There are different kinds of research problems that a life history research project could explore. Here are some examples:

- *Empirical problem:* This research collects data aimed at filling a knowledge gap(s) on a specific issue that was not addressed by previous studies on the topic.
- *Theoretical problem:* This research examines how a theory can be applied, adapted, or modified.
- *Conceptual problem:* This research explores the meaning and application of concepts in specific contexts or examine relationships between concepts.
- *Epistemological problem:* This research project investigates the contradictions or paradoxes in thinking patterns.

- *Action/applied research:* This research addresses a real-world challenge. It may examine practical problems, such as social justice, health problems, or economic issues with the aim of suggesting evidence-based solutions to enhance existing practice.

PURPOSE OF THE STUDY AND RESEARCH QUESTION

After identifying the research problem, it is time to think through the **purpose of the study.** This is a statement that explains the research aims, significance, and expected outputs from the study.

To define the purpose of the study, start with an exploratory research question. The exploratory question may begin with a "why" or "how." You may later refine it into a "what" question to sharpen its focus if necessary. For example, *how do new Black immigrants survive in the United States?* can be converted into *what are the experiences of emigrated Black youth living in the United States?*

Table 2.1 gives examples of research topics and related "how?" questions.

Table 2.1 Types of Research Problems

Type of research problem	Research topic	Research question
Empirical	Examining the impact of migration policies on Black migrants	How do migration policies impact Black migrant communities?
Theoretical	The application of Critical Race Theory to understanding Black migration experiences	How do racism and power structures shape the migration experiences of Black people?
Conceptual	Analysis of the relationship between identity and belonging among Black migrants	How do Black migrants negotiate their experiences of belonging in their host communities?

(Continued)

Table 2.1 (Continued)

Type of research problem	Research topic	Research question
Epistemological and/ methodological	Narratives of Black migration	How can first-person narratives Black migration stories shape our understanding of their experiences
Action/Applied Research	Supports for the integration of Black migrants	How can Black migrants be supported to integrate in their new communities?

Such exploratory questions may be inspired by your own personal or academic interests. For example, it could be an unanswered question from the findings of your previous research project (empirical question). Maybe you want to use the life history method to study an issue that has been previously researched using quantitative or other qualitative methods. It could also be a concern raised by members of the Black community you serve or collaborate with. It could also arise out of a need to contribute to finding a solution to a contemporary social problem (applied research question).

LITERATURE REVIEW

Reviewing literature plays an important role in designing any research project including a life history research project. Armed with your research idea or open-ended question, you will have to review literature related to this topic or idea. While reviewing literature, remember to read critically. Reading critically means engaging the author (Natukunda et al., 2019). Assume that the author of the article or whatever material you are reading is seated in front of you waiting for you to evaluate their writing. As you review the literature, below is a list of questions you can ask yourself and take notes. Here is a structured plan for reviewing literature including concrete steps (Table 2.2).

Table 2.2   Literature Review Steps

Steps	What to consider
1. Identify the literature	• Find the literature—what previous studies have been conducted about this topic or related topics? • Create a system to keep your literature collection organized. You may want to use a reference management tool to do that.
2. Read, summarize and synthesize	• In your own words, summarize the paper/article/chapter by capturing • What is already known about your topic? • The key arguments/debates and key findings. • Which categories of Black people have been studied, and using which methods? • What do previous studies tell us about the experiences of a specific community of Black people and people of African descent?
3. Compare and critique	• Evaluate the strengths and weaknesses of the work • Take note of how different studies relate • What views need further exploration or proof or are contradictory? • Which findings are inconclusive? • Which methods seem unsatisfactory for studying Black communities? • How is this work applicable to your population of interest?
4. Put it all together	• What is known about this topic? • What is unknown about this topic? • What could my research contribute? • What can I contribute to this conversation? • Why do I need to go further in the direction that scholar XYZ took?

Source: Author.

Reviewing the literature will be helpful in terms of strengthening your research idea and potential contribution. However, remember to remain open-minded about your question while focusing on the specific category of Black people and their experiences. Avoid using literature that refers to broader categories like "racialized people," "people of color," and "racial minorities." Although the literature review is crucial for identifying a research topic and uncovering gaps in current understanding, the initial research idea generated at this stage should be viewed as a preliminary one, subject to refinement and adaptation as the research progresses. This is because it will be easier for you to formulate a good research question after exploring the literature in your field.

SAMPLING AND RECRUITMENT

In any research project, sampling is the process of selecting a subset of individuals, groups, communities, locations, cases, etc. from a larger population to include in a study. For a life history research project, this requires the researcher to make choices of location, community, and individuals.

Study site/geographical location. Once the research question has been formulated and the research purpose established, the next step is to select a study location and a study population. While early life history researchers followed an ethnographic design in which many of them chose to conceal their research plans to avoid influencing the behaviors of the community members, disclosing your identity and research aims is important when working with Black people and people of African descent. Their stories are not just stories—they are sacred parts of culture and must be collected, analyzed, and reported ethically.

- Choice of a research location should be informed by *the research problem and research question* you are exploring. For example, if you were studying migration experiences of Black people and people of African descent in North America, it would be best to consider locations where you would find more emigrated Black people. Assuming your study is focusing on educational experiences of young immigrants, you will need a location where you are likely to find a diverse community of Black people and people of African descent.
- Apart from the research question, your *research approach* should also be considered. If you are using the AOST framework,

you should select a location where community members are likely to embrace this approach.

• Finally, consider the *researcher positionality*. How much of an insider or outsider are you to this community based on your ethnicity, age, level of education, world views, ability, gender, sexual orientation? Are you aware of your own biases about this location/community and how you will address them?

All that to say that the choice of your study site is usually guided by your study problem and question, research approach, and researcher positionality, therefore, should be done purposively.

STUDY POPULATION

Now that you have identified a suitable study location, you will need to select and recruit participants. Remember, the process of selecting the groups, categories, or individuals from the general population of interest is called sampling. In life history research, we use the type of sampling categorized as non-probability sampling where study participants are selected on the basis of the researchers' judgment informed by the nature of the research problem and participants, availability (Goodson & Sikes, 2016). The purpose of sampling in a life history study is not to generalize the findings but to achieve depth in terms of the richness of data. In the case of Black people and people of African descent, the sampling process can follow the steps below:

1. Define the **research population**.

   • Identify the specific community of Black people you want to study (e.g., African Americans, Caribbean-Americans, Black mothers, Black high school students).
   • Define the subcategory of focus—assuming you decide to study *African Americans,* what is your population of

focus? Throughout this book, I have been using the example of immigrants. These too have subcategories based on age, country of origin, gender identity, sexuality, geographical location, marital/romantic relationship status, etc. You want to be as specific as possible.

- Let's pick *age* (young people 10–18 years) and *geographical location* (living in Toronto) for our example. As a Canadian, I know that Toronto is a diverse city, and it would be possible to recruit the young people from schools or youth programs.

2. Determine the **sampling frame or a list or pool of potential participants**. For example, now that we are looking for young people, we would have to come up with a list of schools, community organizations serving the youth, etc. Again, this would be informed by what exact category of youth we are looking for. Let us assume that we are looking for unhoused or houseless immigrant youth, we are very unlikely to find these in schools but in organizations/agencies serving unhoused people and unhoused youth. Our task would be to come up with a list of these organizations in a Toronto location. Once we have this list, then we are ready for recruitment.

3. Select a **sampling method**. Common methods used in life history research include the following:

- *Purposive sampling* is a method in which participants are selected based on their characteristics, expertise, or experience (lived or embodied). You need to specify your inclusion criteria. For example, if we are focusing on unhoused young immigrants living in Toronto, our inclusion criteria for purposive sampling would be age (10–18 years), emigrated to Canada, currently not living in a regular home or house (e.g., lives in a temporary shelter, on the streets) in Toronto, willing to participate. In other words, you must select a sampling method that is appropriate for your research question, population and theoretical framework. Although purposive sampling relies on the researchers' choice of inclusion and exclusion criteria, always remember to consider criteria that will enable you to collect data, which will be helpful in terms of answering your question or meeting your research goals.

• *Snowball sampling* is a sampling method where existing participants are requested to refer prospective participants. Snowball sampling can be done in the following steps:

  i. *Initial contact*: The researcher can start by identifying and contacting initial participant such as through a community organization, local leaders, social media. The first participant is taken through the formal recruitment process including explaining the goal of the research and obtaining consent. Consent is a voluntary agreement to participate in the study after being fully informed about the potential risks, benefits, and consequences. You may start with one or two initial participants because not everyone will be able or willing or to refer others. However, remember that you do not need many participants to complete your life history research. Be cautious about the potential risk of recruiting more people than you need for your study.

  ii. *Establish strong "field" relations*: Among Black people and people of African descent, asking participants to refer their acquaintances is not a small task especially if you do not belong to the specific community of interest. Black people and people of African descent in the diaspora have experienced historical trauma, including being offspring of the enslaved, and colonized, and suffering ongoing systemic racism. Historically, Black people and people of African descent have been pathologized, underrepresented in research, or misrepresented in research findings. Some Black communities may have a strong sense of caution when dealing with "outsiders" particularly in research contexts. Remember that even Black people require self-interrogation in some cases. For example, a Black adult studying young people or people who belong to a different socioeconomic status requires doing so ethically and cautiously. Therefore, how you apply snowball sampling to recruit Black people and people of African descent into your study matters. It is important to invest time and effort in building trust with the initial participants and probably their communities before you can request them to refer others.

iii. *Referral:* The first participants will serve as your referrers. At an appropriate time, you may ask them to refer friends, family members, neighbors, or other people they might know who fit the inclusion criteria of the study. Do not be in a hurry to ask them for referrals until you have completed the data collection process with them. To be respectful to the participant, you want to be sure that you do everything right and have a good relationship with each participant before asking them to refer others.

Snowball sampling can be combined with purposive sampling to achieve good results as has been done by some scholars to study Black people and people of African descent (see Kakuru et al., 2024; Moore, 2013; Plaza, 2006; Stitt & Happel-Parkins, 2019). Recruitment can stop when the researcher reaches the point of data saturation or the required number of participants.

TEST YOUR UNDERSTANDING

1. What are the factors to consider when choosing a research site?
   (research problem, research approach, positionality)
2. What are the two things to bear in mind when using purposive sampling?
   (inclusion criteria and purpose of the study)
3. What are the three steps in snowball sampling?
   (initial contact, establish field relations, referral)

LIFE HISTORY RESEARCH APPROACHES

I offer two research approaches that can be used in life history research: narrative inquiry and autoethnography.

NARRATIVE INQUIRY

Narrative inquiry is a qualitative research approach that explores how people construct and share their life experiences through storytelling. It is based on the idea that humans understand their lives through narratives that shape their identities, memories, and social realities. Narrative inquiry examines the meanings behind personal stories, focusing on how individuals frame and narrate their experiences. Narrative inquiry as a research methodology was made popular by Connelly and Clandinin (1990), who were significantly influenced by Dewey (1938). Dewey emphasized the importance of interaction, continuity, and situation in understanding human experience. Narrative inquiry is a nuanced and iterative methodology characterized by an ongoing dialogue between the researcher and participant. Through a process of reciprocal validation, both parties continuously negotiate and refine the meaning of the stories, ensuring that the narrative accounts are accurate, trustworthy, and contextualized (Wang & Geale, 2015). According to Wang and Geale (2015, p. 197), "researchers need to continually discuss the participant's stories with the participant, and reflect on [their] personal, social, and political background. This process shapes how the researcher re-stories the account within the framework." Dewey, as described by Wang and Geale, outlined a three-dimensional narrative structure comprising personal and social interaction aspects of the story-teller, continuity (past, present, and future actions of the storyteller), and situation or place (the physical locations in the storyteller's narrative and how they are related to their experience). This narrative inquiry approach recognizes that participants' stories are embedded in their social contexts, personal experiences, and spatial locations.

Narrative inquiry can serve as a decolonial tool as well as a methodology that respects the oral traditions of Black communities. It empowers participants to confirm their histories, avoiding misrepresentations in outsiders' interpretations of data. Unlike traditional research methods that often impose rigid structures, narrative inquiry values participants' cultural worldviews, making it especially relevant for studying Black people and people of African descent.

Conducting Narrative Inquiry with Black People and People of African Descent

Establish trust and build relationships. Narrative inquiry researchers must recognize that many Black communities still mistrust the research process due to exploitative practices, unethical experiments, and harms inflicted on them, such as the forced sterilization of Black women in the 20th century (Smaw, 2022). Researchers should therefore approach Black community members with humility and intentionally work toward building long-term relationships in order to successfully engage in narrative inquiry.

Use decolonial and culturally grounded methods:

- Incorporate oral traditions, storytelling circles, and story revisiting. Story revisiting, a significant aspect of narrative inquiry, is a process where storytellers reexamine and reinterpret their personal narratives (Wang & Geale, 2015). This methodology allows for a deeper understanding of experiences by acknowledging that meanings can evolve over time. In the narrative approach, the stories allow participants to speak of their experiences without externally imposed constraints (Wang & Geale, 2015, p. 196).

- Analyze narratives within social and historical contexts by identifying themes, struggles, and resilience in Black diasporic people's experiences. Examine how personal stories intersect with racial histories, migration, colonialism, and identity formation and purpose to recognize silences and omissions, because what people do not say can be just as important as what they say.

- Ethically represent and share findings. For example, it is important to ensure that Black people are not pathologized or reduced to victimhood. Offer community ownership of the research and ensure that the findings remain accessible to participants.

AUTOETHNOGRAPHY

Autoethnography is a research practice that emphasizes the importance of personal experience and narrative in understanding human life (Bochner, 2017). It is a method of collecting life history data in which the researcher reflects on and writes about their own life experiences. Bochner (2017, p. 72) considers "memory work" to be "the lifeline of autoethnography." Thus, autoethnographic writers share common tenets such as valuing stories, centering personal experience, and engaging in critical research practices (Adams et al., 2017). Autoethnographic researchers do not simply share stories about their life experiences. They aim to "speak against, or provide alternatives to, dominant, taken-for-granted, and harmful cultural scripts, stories, and stereotypes" (Adams et al., 2017, p. 3). Autoethnography is a powerful research approach for studying Black people and people of African descent, whose experiences are more often than not either minoritized or pathologized. It is often taken up by racialized scholars as it relates to their cultural ways of being. It is a transformative research practice commonly used in identity scholarship as well as in challenging power relations. For example, Griffin (2012) conducted a study to investigate the intersection between Black feminist theory and autoethnography to understand the experiences of Black women. Griffin called this method Black feminist autoethnography (BFA). Through her research, Griffin demonstrated how she reclaimed her voice and challenged dominant images attributed to Black womanhood. She opines that BFA is a powerful tool for Black women to communicate their struggles and claim their identities.

Autoethnography is a flexible and creative method that can be innovatively used to study marginalized communities (Gulamhusein, 2024). For example, Gulamhusein (2024, p. 7) used an autoethnographic approach called the "third-wave dervish methodology" to deepen her understanding of "living in the in-between of social spaces as an Ismaili Muslim woman in Canada." Through autoethnography, experiences across the lifespan can be explored that then highlights the intersectional, complex, and often unconsciously negotiated ways that marginalized people move through their days. Gulamhusein shares stories from early childhood to young adulthood, all reflecting experiences of subtle racism that altered her understanding of self, belonging, and the ways she shows up for others. As Ellis (2009) notes, autoethnography can place the scholar in vulnerable, dangerous, creative, and rebellious spaces. Black people and people of African scholars are constantly in such spaces in scholarship, and autoethnography provides them with power over their own stories/narratives/experiences.

Autoethnographic narratives can be used to bring our attention to the fact that daily lifestyles and practices can be used as tools for self-expression and resisting systemic oppression. Osei (2019), for example, drawing on Black feminism and fashion, examined her experiences as a Ghanaian-Cameroonian-American Black woman. In her reflection, Osei looked at fashion and material culture as forms of sociopolitical expression and activism. She reflected on her childhood memories of sewing and her mother's gardening practices. Based on this reflection, Osei illustrated how these activities served as actions of resistance against racial and gendered oppression. Osei asserts that self-fashioning and aesthetic expression are effective tools to reclaim Black womanhood and to navigate the complexities of identity within diasporic contexts.

In another example, Slay (2023) used critical race theory and Black feminist perspectives to investigate the psychological stress experienced by Black women faculty in academia. Reflecting on her personal experience, Slay identified several psychologically stressing experiences faced by Black female academics at the University of Kentucky in the United States.

Despite offering insights on how various individual experiences can explain the broader social landscape, autoethnography, like any other method, can be challenging in some ways. A central challenge is that when telling one's self-story, it is easy to involve others. This is because "human beings are relational beings, and thus every story of the self is a story of relations with others" (Bochner, 2017, p. 76). It is therefore important to pay attention to relational and procedural ethics (e.g., Adams et al., 2017; Bochner, 2017; Lapadat, 2017) as a way to address some of the weaknesses inherent in the method. For example, Edwards (2021) suggests consideration of the ethics of self. According to

Edwards, ethics of the self is when the researcher investigates their own experiences but with careful attention to not harming their emotions and self-reputation.

Steps in planning and collecting autoethnographic data as a Black researcher might include these:

1. Reflect and identify the research topic.
2. Reflect on your personal experiences and identify a significant event, issue, or theme that you would like to explore. Think through how your personal experiences intersect with broader cultural, social, or historical contexts.
3. Define the research question or focus to guide your research.
4. Collect personal data through:
   - Reflexive journaling or diary-keeping
   - Writing autobiographical accounts or memoirs
   - Interviewing family members, friends, or others who have knowledge of your experiences
   - Identifying and analyzing personal artifacts, such as photographs, letters, or other objects.

Remember that autoethnographic research is a highly personal and reflexive process. Be prepared to engage in ongoing self-reflection and critique throughout your research journey.

SUMMARY

In this chapter, I have described how to formulate a research question, including the different types of questions one can explore in a life history research project with Black communities. I outlined the step-by-step process for conducting a literature review. The chapter also described the process of selecting Black communities, individual participants, and their location. Once you have solidified your research questions, sampling, and methodology, the next step is data collection, which is the topic of Chapter 3.

FURTHER READINGS

Chang, H. (2008). *Autoethnography as method.* Routledge.

Clandinin, D. J. (2016). *Engaging in narrative inquiry.* Routledge. https://doi.org/10.4324/9781315429618

Conyers, L. Jr., & Conyers, J. L. (Eds.). (2016). *Qualitative methods in Africana studies: An interdisciplinary approach to examining Africana phenomena.* University Press of America Inc.

Harris, D. J. (2020). *Literature review and research design: A guide to effective research practice.* Routledge, Taylor & Francis Group.

CHAPTER 3
Life History Data Collection

I hope you are excited to have come this far. In this chapter, you get to learn how to collect life history data from Black people and people of African descent. Remember that life history is rooted four key urgencies (Denzin & Lincoln, 2011). These are the urgency of speaking, which empowers narrators to share their life experiences; the urgency of being heard, where individuals' stories are made available for others to acknowledge; the urgency of collective stories, which connects personal narratives to broader social groups with similar experiences, highlighting social justice practices; and the urgency of public dialogue, where these stories are brought into public attention, sparking discussion and action. These four urgencies are important considerations when collecting data from Black diasporic communities.

PREPARATION STAGE

This stage includes several factors to consider prior to embarking on the data collection process, such as having a clearly defined research question, going through ethical clearance procedures and other logistical considerations depending on the nature of data collection method.

Decolonize Your Gaze

Before you begin conducting research with Black people and
people of African descent, it is essential to rethink your perspective. Conventional research perspectives can carry biases that
overlook the rich complexity and diversity within Black communities. A worthwhile goal is to decolonize your mind and
cleanse yourself of all potential anti-Blackness, supremacy,
saviorism, and racism, to name a few. To achieve this goal, some
concrete steps include the following:

- *Reflect on your assumptions about Blackness.* Take time to
  assess your own ontological assumptions, personal beliefs,
  biases, and preconceived notions of blackness and Black
  people. Consider how your background influences your perspective and how this could potentially impact the knowledge
  you seek and what you intend to do with it.
- *Commit to continuous learning.* Educate yourself by seeking
  out information about the communities you wish to understand. Focus on resources that center Black voices and
  experiences. Open yourself to a broader understanding and
  appreciation of the unique histories, cultures, and narratives
  of Black communities. Decolonizing your perspective is an
  ongoing journey. Stay curious and open to new ideas as you
  continuously learn and unlearn.
- *Commit to promoting inclusivity.* Ensure that you include a
  diverse range of Black ethnicities, voices, experiences, identities, sexualities, especially those that are often overlooked.
- *Resist the savior complex.* Whether you are a Black
  researcher or an ally with good intentions, acknowledge and
  address your privilege and power and avoid positioning
  yourself as the "mighty savior." Avoiding saviorism means
  recognizing the agency of Black people and communities as
  capable of navigating their circumstances. This requires
  critically examining the power dynamics and committing to
  collaborative, equitable, and inclusive research practices.

Taking steps to intentionally decolonize your gaze not only enriches your research but honors the agency of Black voices in the stories you seek to uncover. This is a call for researchers to critically examine and challenge their own biases and assumptions before conducting research on Black people and communities of African descent.

Participant Orientation

Orienting your participants can be done in several ways. One way is by sharing a research concept with the selected participants before the interview. This process gives some level of control to the participant since they can be given a few minutes to collect their thoughts or think through their story in advance instead of being put on the spot. Another benefit of preparing the participants this way is that it increases the researcher's chances of getting richer stories in terms of **depth** and **breadth**.

By **depth** I mean the level of detail, nuance, and complexity. Before collecting data, you should take the time to prepare the possible interview questions and probes. In a study about Black activism in Greece, Gousis and Gill (2023) outlined their interview questions and used these to orient the participants. This approach is helpful in terms of helping participants to know how far they can go with their stories. If you put yourself in the participant's shoes, you can better understand the importance of orienting participants, as I did (see Box 3.1).

BOX 3.1 IMPORTANCE OF ORIENTING STUDY PARTICIPANTS

As a young researcher, I served as a volunteer in a school while conducting ethnographic research for my doctoral thesis. One of the kids, named Chad, fulfilled the inclusion

(Continued)

---

criteria for the life history interview. Chad was living with a disability that impacted his school experience. Toward the end of the interview, I asked Chad about his classroom experience. After he answered, Chad asked me about my own middle school experience. I remember pausing for a moment because I wanted to ensure I gave him a satisfactory and relevant response. This interaction taught me the importance of preparing participants for such discussions. I was not sure why Chad was interested in my middle school experience. I needed time to sift through my experiences and decide what to share in an ethical way, especially given my positionality as an able-bodied, educated person conducting research in a low-income community.

After orienting the participant, the researcher goes through the in-depth interview using open-ended questions. A participant prepared in advance is likely to provide more anecdotes and deeper emotional reflections and insights.

Breadth refers to the scope and range of perspectives and ideas. For example, a participant who is prepared is likely to cite more than two or three events they consider as having been significant in their life story, while an unprepared one may give only one. Preparing the participant is not commonly done in conventional life history research. However, doing so helps us to work toward a more inclusive and equitable representation of Black life histories. We want to collect data that honor the complexity, diversity, and richness of Black experiences in the diaspora. One of the significant benefits of this research approach is that it amplifies the voices of individual Black people and people of African descent that might otherwise remain muted, excluded, or distorted by traditional research methods. This amplification of their voices provides a platform for their personal narratives and experiences to be shared and valued.

Ethical Issues in Conducting Life History Research

Conducting research with Black communities ethically is a challenge every researcher must take with humility given the exploitative and unethical research practices they have endured in the past. Apart from the standard ethics approval procedures, life history research with Black people requires nuanced ethics considerations that should be made upfront. This is because the stories of Black communities are sacred.

BOX 3.2   BLACK STORIES ARE SACRED

To people of African descent, life histories and oral histories are not just data. Storying is a cultural phenomenon and a vessel for passing down Black Indigenous knowledge such as cultural values, traditions, and practices of care from generation to generation. Therefore, conducting life history research among Black people and people of African descent requires essential preparatory work, which is not often covered in traditional research textbooks. Black people in the diaspora face daily experiences of racism that serve as a constant reminder of the injustices inflicted on their ancestors.

Any researcher trying to act and behave ethically while conducting research with Black people will need to consider some general points.

- *Understand the context.* Black people are of different kinds, and each community has its unique historical context, experiences, and expectations. Merely obtaining ethics approval based on Euro-Western guidelines does not guarantee that you will act ethically if you do not have a nuanced understanding of the specific category of Black people and people of African descent relevant for your study. According to McKeever (2000, p. 101), conducting ethical research can sometimes look like a game of snakes and ladders where you have to "cling to the ladders of the oppressed while trying to avoid the snakes." This metaphorical expression suggests that conducting ethical research can be complex and challenging, where researchers must navigate difficult situations and power dynamics. The ladders represent opportunities, allies, or strategies that support the research and amplify the voices of oppressed groups such as Black people. "Clinging to the ladders" means holding onto these opportunities and alliances to ensure the research is conducted ethically and responsibly. The snakes symbolize biases or oppressive systems that can undermine the research's integrity or harm the communities involved. "Avoiding the snakes" means being aware of the potential harms and taking steps to mitigate them. Life history researchers of Black people and people of African descent must go beyond merely obtaining ethics approval. They must intentionally learn the context and remain vigilant, strategic, and committed to practicing Black community ethos in research.

- *Purpose of the study.* The researcher's positionality and epistemological beliefs determine whether the project and the conclusions will be emancipatory or harmful based on how the research is designed and implemented. Black people and people of African descent continue to suffer the consequences of anti-Blackness, racism, labeling, and othering, and their narratives are characterized by a rhetoric of pathology in many research reports. Being ethical begins having an "Afro-emancipatory" (Jean-Pierre et al., 2024, pp. 7–8) purpose for the study. According to Jean-Pierre et al. (2024), one of the tenets of Afro-emancipatory research is that it should target the liberation of Afro-descendant people, who should fully participate in the study. Some researchers conduct life history research just to satisfy their intellectual curiosity. Indeed, according to Goodson and Sikes (2016, p. 73), the life history method is best suited for researchers who are curious about "the minutiae of others' lives" and skilled at listening attentively. However, when it comes to conducting research within Black and African diasporic communities, I firmly believe that mere curiosity is insufficient motivation. This applies to all researchers and students regardless of their racial or ethnic origin—whether they are of Black, Brown, white or other non-white identity. While having a deep interest is necessary, researchers must consider how their findings will contribute positively and meaningfully to the Black community.

- *Black people's involvement.* Not all researchers are suited for life history research with Black people ethically and with care. Again, referring to another characteristic of Jean-Pierre et al.'s (2024) Afro-emancipatory qualitative research framework, all phases of ethical research should be led by Black people.
- *Interview location.* In conventional qualitative research, the researcher usually wields all the power. They indirectly assume that they will meet the participant in their home or workplace or invite them to a neutral location to complete the interview. In most cases, the participant is not given the option to decide where they want to be interviewed. Researchers working with Black communities should endeavor to offer the participant the option to determine the time and location of the interview. According to the AOTS framework (Osei-Tutu, 2021b, 2021a, 2023), story gathering/telling among Black communities is done in a "fireside" space. In many Black communities, there are dedicated spaces where people prefer to gather to drink and eat (usually spicy food). If such a space exists, you will not know whether your participant would prefer to meet there unless you become intentional about finding this information. Therefore, researchers from all backgrounds should intentionally offer participants a choice of meeting location that feels comfortable and familiar to them.

- *Comply with local protocols.* You also want to ensure that you comply with any traditions and rituals for meeting with specific communities. For example, in the traditional African setting, visitors seeking a favor from the head of a family or clan had to come with a pot of local brew/beer or a "handshake." This practice still exists in many communities, but the kind of brew varies from community to community. Due to the perpetuation of anti-Blackness, some Black people may not openly demand that you comply with their protocols when you approach them to participate in your study. The onus is on the researcher to find out upfront whether such protocols exist and, if so, what they entail. This is the time to ask the prospective participants if there are any forms or documents that need to be signed before starting the interview.

- *Practice situated ethics* or seek consent on an ongoing basis. Apart from adhering to procedural ethics as required by the research ethics committee, life history research with Black communities requires situated ethics (Jellema et al., 2024). Practicing situated ethics means seeking consent on a continuous basis as needed. During the research process, you should regularly check in with the participant(s) to ensure that you still have their permission to continue. Sometimes they just want a break, or they may want to withdraw their consent altogether. It is therefore important not to take the initial consent for granted (Table 3.1).

Table 3.1   Key Ethical Issues in Conducting Life History Research With Black Communities

Points to consider	Practical application of the life history research process
Understand the context	Actively prioritize supportive alliances while avoiding biases and oppressive acts, behaviors, and systems.
Purpose of the study	Ensure that your findings will contribute positively to the Black community of focus.

Points to consider	Practical application of the life history research process
Black people's involvement	Let Black people or people of African descent lead.
Interview location	Find out whether there is a fireside space or any other preferred location.
Comply with local protocols	Educate yourself about any unwritten or silent community protocols.
Practice situated ethics	Regularly check in to reconfirm consent/ assent.

Source: Author.

ENTERING THE FIELD

Entering the field in researching Black people and people of African descent is not a one-time event; it is a process. The researcher considers several steps during this stage. The following tips may be useful.

- *Establish rapport with the participants.* This includes making effective initial contact with participants and creating an atmosphere where they feel comfortable or not threatened. Establishing rapport is an art; there is no blueprint to follow. While conducting life history research with Black communities, the researcher must remember that the stories they are seeking are not simply data. For example, a researcher aiming to collect data from a married person must work on establishing trust with both spouses. Some stories belong to the entire family or clan, and if one member of the family is unhappy, it could impact the story you are seeking from another member of that family. Again, the researcher must continuously reflect on their positionality throughout this step and intentionally avoid anti-Blackness tendencies.
- *Ask probing questions.* Prepare a list of guiding questions but remember to "speak in modest amounts" and remain "nondirective" (Yin, 2016, p. 144). You must allow the

participant time to tell their story while probing only where necessary.

- *Revisit stories.* Normally, researchers voice-record interview data, take field notes, and return to the community to validate their findings. The participants rarely have access to the recordings or transcripts of their interviews. Conducting Afrocentric life history research with Black people and people of African descent demands that we validate the findings at the level of the individual. After the first interview, it is important to share the recording and the transcript with the participant. Let them sit with it for a while and decide whether they want to review it or not. If they decide to review it, find out whether they are comfortable with the transcript or whether they want to revise it, clarify, fill gaps, or delete some pieces.

- *Take notes and ask questions.* Many researchers take notes in the process of interviewing. Due to the unequal power relations, researchers always control the process. They pause to take notes of whatever they find relevant or important to the study. However, participants are rarely given the option to take notes or ask questions. Allowing participants sufficient time to take notes and ask questions is essential for building relationships, as well as for demonstrating respect and ethical conduct.

DATA COLLECTION METHODS

A wide variety of methods can be used to collect life history data. These include detailed autobiographical accounts, diaries, and letters from individuals, and interviews (Goodson, 2001). These methods seek to construct a comprehensive narrative of a person's life. Other data collection methods include life and oral histories, autobiographical and biographical data time-lines, calendars, artifacts (including objects such as images or nontangible data such as music). Before jumping into the intricacies of data collection, let us remember that historically, the stories and experiences of Black communities have been marginalized, distorted, invisibilized, minoritized, and ignored in scholarly literature. Research conducted about Black communities by non-Black scholars sometimes prioritizes deficit narratives of violence, disease, and suffering, and Black people have been framed as low income, rebellious, rowdy, and the like. Additionally, it is important to note that being Black does not imply that researchers have no need for self-interrogation. All researchers have a responsibility to acknowledge and challenge the deficit narratives and power dynamics that have shaped the creation and mobilization of knowledge about Black people and people of African descent. Decolonizing the collection of life history data requires us to center the voices, perspectives, and experiences of diverse Black people. It requires us to adopt a critical and reflexive approach to our research, acknowledging our own positionality and biases. Additionally, it requires us to diverge from the conventional extractive methods of collecting life history data. In the field of Africana studies, always remember that life history research cannot be easily proceduralized or conducted in a standardized way (Goodson & Sikes, 2016).

The following sections describe some methods in detail, with examples of research with Black people and people of African descent.

Interviewing

Life history data from Black people and people of African descent can be collected through two major types of interviews— life stories and oral stories, and in-depth interviews.

Life Stories and Oral Histories

Life story refers to a data collection method in which an individual shares about their past life experiences. Shopes (2011) suggests that oral history is as follows:

- a narration obtained through an interview—not simply personal memoirs
- recorded or stored and archived
- contextualized in history
- a subjective interpretation of the interviewee's past experiences
- a detailed oral account of the past.

Life story interviews aim to understand how individuals make sense of their lives. The emphasis in life stories varies across groups and topics. For example, in research exploring identity, older individuals tend to share stories that integrate past experiences into a cohesive narrative, while younger individuals focus on changes and transitions to convey their ongoing identity formation (McLean, 2008).

Apart from life stories, **oral history** data are very useful in life history research. Oral history data can be collected concurrently during storytelling. It involves the collection of oral data such as songs, legends, myths, proverbs, and more. Much of the Black culture and knowledge is passed on from person to person and generation to generation, usually by word of mouth. Some of this culture is transmitted through music and proverbs. The researcher can intentionally collect a wide range of orally transmitted materials through interviews. Among Black communities, oral history data are considered very sacred because oral stories honor our memory (Mucina, 2011). However, if the researcher builds enough rapport with the participants, they will likely volunteer the data in the process of telling stories. Oral history from Black communities can better be collected within the African oral traditional storytelling (AOTS) framework in the fireside space (Osei-Tutu, 2021a). Oral history data sometimes belong to an entire community or family or clan. Before embarking on collecting such sacred oral history data from people of African descent, researchers should ensure they are conforming to cultural protocols of the communities they are studying. If they are outsiders, they must educate themselves about the historical and cultural contexts of the communities being studied.

In-Depth Interviews

In-depth interviews are a cornerstone of life history research, offering a unique window into the complexities of human experience. By engaging in open-ended conversational exchanges, researchers can gather rich, contextualized data that reveals the nuances of Black people's lives. Through in-depth interviews, researchers can explore the intricacies of human memory, identity, and meaning making, gaining insight into the ways in which individuals narrate and construct their lives. In-depth interviews allow participants to share their stories in their own words, thereby providing a platform for voices that might otherwise remain unheard. The researcher should allow the flow of the conversation to be controlled by the participant without making unnecessary interruptions (Goodson, 2016). Such autonomy enables the participant to order and sequence their stories in ways they want.

Although in-depth interviews are important in all disciplines, when it comes to life history research within Africana studies, they must be adapted to the specific cultural, historical, and social contexts that shape the lives of Black and people of African descent. For instance, ethical considerations must be made to ensure that interviews are conducted with sensitivity to power dynamics and historical traumas, particularly given the legacy of colonization, slavery, and systemic racism. Building trust is also paramount. The need for researchers to engage with communities respectfully and collaboratively, while understanding the importance of reciprocity in these relationships cannot be over-emphasized. This method of interviewing should acknowledge the complexity and agency of individuals, recognizing the participants as active agents in the narration of their own stories. This is particularly important among Black people whose voices are not always centered in academic research. Allowing the participant to lead can potentially strengthen the trust and relationship between the researcher and the participant, leading to high-quality interview data.

Now that we understand the two ways of collecting interview data; let us look at some approaches that have been used to collect life history data using oral life stories or in-depth interviews from Black people and people of African descent.

a.   *McAdams life history interview protocol*

The life story interview (McAdams, 2008) is a data collection tool that focuses on significant life events, themes, and personal significance. The research tool was designed to explore an individual's life narrative by identifying key life events, themes, and personal meaning. The interview consists of several structured sections, including life chapters, key scenes, future aspirations, personal challenges, and ideological beliefs. Participants recount pivotal moments such as high and low points, turning points, childhood memories, and wisdom experiences. Additionally, the interview investigates personal values, political and social views, and the overarching theme of the individual's life story. The goal is to understand how people construct meaning from their experiences and how these narratives shape identity. While applicable to other disciplines, it is specifically invaluable for collecting data within the context of Africana and African studies. This protocol has been used by various scholars including Myrie et al. (2022), whose research investigated the topic of finding Blackness in music among young Black adults.

Box 3.3 presents a summary of the tool as adapted from McAdams (2008) including the steps to follow and the kind of data you can collect.

BOX 3.3   MCADAMS LIFE STORY INTERVIEW

Introduction: Introduce yourself and the purpose of the study and give the participant an opportunity to ask questions. Seek and obtain consent as necessary.

A. Life chapters

Ask the participant to tell the story of their life as if it was a book divided into 2–7 chapters. The participant should describe each chapter in about 20 minutes.

B. Scenes in the life story

After describing the overall outline of their life, ask the participant to focus on key themes or scenes that stand out in the story. "A key scene would be an event or specific incident that took place at a particular time and place" (McAdams, 2008). Ask the participant to describe what, when, where, and who, as well as why they consider this to be an important scene. For each scene, probe for the following:

1. The high point—the happiest or most fulfilling moment.
2. The low point—the most difficult or challenging experience.
3. The turning point—a key moment that changed the direction of their life.
4. Positive childhood memory—an early memory from that stands out in a positive way.
5. Negative childhood memory—an early memory from that stands out in a negative way.

(Continued)

6. Vivid adult memory—important memory not yet described.

7. Wisdom event—a time when they gained an important life lesson.

8. Religious, spiritual, or mystical experience—any significant religious or spiritual episode.

C. Future Script

Participants imagine their future by describing what they believe their life will look like five, ten, or more years from now. They discuss their hopes, dreams, and expected life trajectory.

D. Challenges and Personal Struggles

Here, individuals reflect on major life challenges, obstacles, and struggles, including how they have faced adversity and whether they feel they have grown from these experiences.

E. Personal Ideology

This section explores the participant's guiding beliefs, values, and ideology. It includes discussions on religion, spirituality, morality, and political or social views that have shaped their life.

F. Life Theme

Participants are asked to summarize the overarching theme of their life—what their story is ultimately about and how they define their personal journey.

G. Other

What else should I know to understand your story?

This life story data collection tool is a flexible example that can be adapted to suit one's research needs within the tradition of Africana and African studies. Be mindful that it may not be universally applicable; consider your participants' specific context and experiences. For instance, when exploring forced migration experiences among Black immigrants, or Black people who are incarcerated, be sensitive to how you inquire about their future script. It is essential to prioritize the ethical principle of "do no harm" and avoid causing unnecessary distress or trauma.

b. *Open-ended interviewing*

This is a type of interview where the researcher uses broad, open-ended questions to collect life history data. This approach to life history research with Black and people of African descent is well suited to Africana studies. This is because of the discipline's commitment to centering African epistemologies and honoring Black people's experiences, voices, diverse cultures and ways of knowing as valid rich knowledge (McDougal, 2014). As one example, Pabon (2017) used Siedman's (2006) interview protocol to design interview questions to understand Black male teachers' recollections of suffering as Black youth in US public schools. Siedman's protocol is presented in Box 3.4 below (as quoted by Pabon, 2017, p. 780, who also quotes Faraday & Plummer, 1979).

BOX 3.4   INTERVIEW PROTOCOL

"My first interview began with the statement, 'Can you tell me about your childhood? Your parents? Your family and their education?' I then asked, 'Can you tell me about your education? Schooling? Teachers?' In addition, I asked the participants to elaborate on moments that seemed to be significant in their schooling experience by asking,

(Continued)

'Can you tell me about a time when x happened in school? What happened? Why does this moment stand out?' Finally, I asked, 'How do you understand what brought you to teaching?' In addition to these broad questions, I used probing questions such as 'What do you mean by that' and 'What was that experience like for you' to further encourage participants to 'interpret, understand and define the world[s] around them' (Faraday and Plummer, 1979, 776)" (Pabon, 2017, p. 780).

Open-ended interviewing is a powerful strategy for collecting life history data. Pabon (2017) formulated open-ended questions that were strategically phrased to encourage storytelling. Here is a list of examples of open-ended guiding questions that you can use to collect data about any topic.

- Tell me the story of your life beginning with your earliest memories up to now—how did you end up at this point in life?
- Tell me more about yourself (early childhood, hobbies, growing up, education, spirituality, friends).
- Tell me about your family (parents, siblings, members of extended family, if any).
- Tell me about your experience with [whatever the research is about].
- Tell me about the most significant event in your life—what are you most proud of?
- Is there anything you regret that you wish to share (e.g., the most disappointing time of your life)?

As a researcher, you can tweak and use these open-ended questions to generate a story of a participant's life on the research topic of choice. Another list of questions, which Osseo-Asare (2017) used in a study that investigated early literacy development for 4- to 8-year-olds using life stories of Ghanaian teachers and postcolonial theory, provides a useful example:

- Where were you born, and where did you live as a child?
- What is the history of your education before training college?
- Why did you choose to become a teacher, and which training college did you attend?
- What teaching certificate do you hold?
- What memories do you have of your training as a teacher?
- Which classes did you teach, and why?
- How did you find your first experience of teaching?
- Which language did you use in teaching, why, and how did you have to use it?
- What other language policy do you know of?
- What is your understanding of the language policy?
- What was your school's reaction to the language policy?
- What are some of the sociocultural changes that took place during your education and the time of your teaching lower grade?
- What are your memories of teaching lower grade? (Osseo-Asare, 2017, p. 82)

RECORDING DATA IN LIFE HISTORY RESEARCH

The life history method, like many other qualitative research methods, requires the researcher to develop strong multitasking skills. At one moment during the data collection process, the researcher is likely to find themselves asking questions, listening attentively, and recording the conversation while taking notes. Data recording is one of the most important stages of any life history research project. Data may be recorded as field notes or through voice recording.

Field Notes

When writing field notes, the researcher should take note of the participant's body language/posture, facial expressions, and emotions and briefly describe the interview setting. Pabon (2017) used field notes to capture the physical appearance, gestures, and disposition of each participant. Such notes are helpful centering the humanness of each participant in the research process. Some scholars (e.g., Smith Lee & Robinson, 2019) use a "feelings chart" to document emotions during an interview. Pabon (2017) used a fieldwork diary to take note of the interview settings and encounters. Such a diary is particularly helpful at the data analysis stage because it enables the researcher to analyze details over and above the stories told by the participants (Gousis & Gill, 2023).

Voice Recording

In the field of Africana studies, while written field notes can be powerful sources of data, it is not always possible to take notes that would cover the entire story. Field notes often fall short of capturing the full depth of the speakers' experiences including emotions. Thanks to technology, it is easy to voice-record an entire conversation or story. Voice recording offers an additional advantage to the researcher: They can analyze the words as well as the tone and intonations of the participants. In some Black communities, how loud one is speaking varies according to the speaker's emotional state. Recording voice adds layers of meaning to the discourse that written notes might overlook such as tone, inflection, and silences all of which hold cultural and emotional importance (Denzin & Lincoln, 2011).

SUMMARY

This chapter has described the methods for collecting life history data. Before you start collecting data, it is important that you are well prepared. This important stage includes decolonizing your gaze or the lenses through which you approach the work. The preparation stage also includes participant orientation and solidifying your ethical considerations. The chapter presented data collection methods, including life and oral stories and in-depth interviews. The life story captures a participant's entire life, including significant events, experiences, and turning points. The in-depth interview is a more guided method in which the interviewer focuses on a specific topic of interest. For example, it can be a participant's migration story or a childhood story with focused themes and events. The chapter also presented ideas on recording your data through field notes or voice recording. The next chapter will address how to analyze the data in life history research.

FURTHER READINGS

Bönisch-Brednich, B. (Ed.). (2023). *Migrant narratives: Storytelling as agency, belonging, and community*. Taylor & Francis.

Mucina, D. D. (2011). Story as research methodology. *AlterNative: An International Journal of Indigenous Peoples*, 7(1), 1–14. https://doi.org/10.1177/117718011100700101

Sikes, P., & Goodson, I. (2016). What have you got when you've got a life story? In I. Goodson, A. Antikainen, P. Sikes, & M. Andrews (Eds.), *The Routledge international handbook on narrative and life history* (1st ed., pp. 60–71). Routledge. https://doi-org.ezproxy.library.uvic.ca/10.4324/9781315768199

Toliver, S. R. (2021). *Recovering Black storytelling in qualitative research: Endarkened storywork*. Routledge.

CHAPTER 4
Data Analysis

INTRODUCTION

In this chapter, I offer ideas on how to analyze life history data collected from Black people and people of African descent. I describe how to apply a modified version of reflexive thematic analysis (RTA; Braun & Clarke, 2019, 2020) to analyze life history data collected from Black people and people of African descent from the perspective of Africana and African studies.

RTA was developed as a response to scholars' misconceptions about thematic analysis (Braun & Clarke, 2006; Clarke & Braun, 2014) as applied in the field of psychology. RTA is a flexible and interpretative approach to qualitative data analysis that enables researchers to identify and analyze patterns and themes within a data set (Byrne, 2022). According to Byrne (2022), this approach acknowledges the researcher's active role in knowledge production. The codes generated through RTA represent the researcher's interpretations of meaningful patterns across the data set. According to Braun and Clarke (2019, p. 594), "quality reflexive TA is not about following procedures 'correctly' (or about 'accurate' and 'reliable' coding, or achieving consensus between coders), but about the researcher's reflective and thoughtful engagement with their data and their reflexive and thoughtful engagement with the analytic process."

Braun and Clarke's (2020) RTA is composed of six phases: (1) familiarization with the data through reading it to identify information relevant to the purpose of the study, (2) generating initial codes, (3) generating themes, (4) reviewing potential themes, (5) defining and naming the themes, and (6) producing the report. A key aspect of RTA is its reflexive nature. Unlike other forms of thematic analysis, RTA acknowledges that researchers play an active role in shaping themes, rather than simply discovering them, through their interpretations. This approach encourages a nuanced and contextual understanding of the data. RTA is distinct from other forms of thematic analysis, such as coding reliability, thematic analysis, and codebook thematic analysis. While these approaches rely on structured and predefined frameworks, RTA allows for a more fluid and iterative process of coding and theme development. This flexibility makes RTA particularly useful in studies that require deep interpretive engagement with the data.

WHY RTA IS NOT ENOUGH

While RTA is a powerful approach for analyzing qualitative data generally, I worry that it over-relies on the researcher's ability to thoughtfully reflect on the data. Researchers of Black people and people of African descent should be cautious about reflecting on the data and drawing conclusions based on their own reflections and thoughtfulness. In African and Africana studies, we need an approach that recognizes that subjective interpretation of the data based only on the researcher's perspectives and assumptions is disempowering and dismissive of the experiences and knowledge of the communities being studied.

Applying the RTA in African and Africana studies requires a more nuanced approach to data analysis. One that acknowledges the limitations and potential harm of relying solely on the researcher's perspectives and assumptions, particularly when working with Black people and people of African descent. An approach is required that prioritizes the perspectives and experiences of Black communities in the data analysis process and ensures their voices are heard in the findings. In recognizing their own biases and assumptions, the researcher becomes more accountable for the impact of their work on marginalized communities.

HESHIMA: AN AFROCENTRIC METHODOLOGY FOR RESEARCHING BLACK LIVES

I am proposing the *Heshima* Afrocentric framework for conducting and analyzing life history research with Black people and people of African descent. The word *Heshima* originates from Swahili—a Bantu language spoken in East Africa—and it means "dignity" (Warren et al., 2017, p. 2) or respect as used in this book. In many African and Black diasporic communities, Heshima applies to every relationship. Respect means treating everyone and everything with care, listening to each other, talking politely, and not offending anyone. The historical context of Black people's experiences is crucial to understanding the significance of Heshima. Heshima is rooted in the fact that anti-Blackness, which is a phenomenon characterized by the reading of Black bodies as "criminal, animalistic, or deviant" (Warren, 2021, p. 8), is often used as justification for anti-Black oppression. Anti-Blackness underlies all violence toward Black people, and harm shows up in research practices and theorizing about Black people and people of African descent. Heshima is deeply rooted in ubuntu philosophy, while focusing on vigilance, care, and accountability in research. It prioritizes knowledge production that affirms Black existence, resilience, and liberation. Heshima emphasizes relationality, storytelling, and transformative justice for Black people and people of African descent. The Heshima framework aims to enhance decolonial and anti-colonial research practices while fostering Black-focused epistemologies, theorizing, and analysis.

The history of transatlantic slave trade, colonialism, and systemic racism have resulted in anti-Blackness, or the dehumanization and marginalization of Black people. The effects of anti-blackness, and racism, are perpetuated through various forms of oppression, including economic exploitation, cultural erasure, and epistemological violence, with far-reaching consequences affecting every aspect of Black life from education and health care to economic opportunities and social mobility. Traditional research methodologies have often been used to reinforce colonial narratives, perpetuate stereotypes, and justify anti-Blackness and anti-Black racial oppression. Researchers have frequently approached Black communities with a saviorist, paternalistic attitude, seeking to "study" and "help" them without truly understanding their experiences, perspectives, or needs. Heshima seeks to challenge and dismantle these traditional research methodologies by centering Black lived experiences, communal knowledge, and culturally responsive narratives. This analytical framework recognizes that Black people are not objects of study but rather subjects with agency, expertise, and knowledge. Heshima prioritizes the voices, perspectives, and experiences of Black people and communities, ensuring that the analysis is respectful, dignified, and honorable. As we move forward, it is essential to prioritize Heshima and other Afrocentric, decolonial research methodologies that seek to center diverse Black epistemologies, voices, experiences, perspectives, and cultures in research. Below are alternative approaches to ensure more inclusive, culturally responsive, and non-deficit-oriented research data analysis when using reflexive thematic analysis.

Decolonial and Afrocentric Methodologies

These approaches challenge Eurocentric research norms and prioritize knowledge systems rooted in African and diasporic worldviews. Decoloniality critiques the persistent legacies of colonialism in academic practices, urging scholars to reassess the power structures inherent in knowledge production. Decolonial thought stemmed from the recognition that colonialism not only restructured economies and societies but also significantly influenced academic discourse, often privileging Western narratives (Mignolo & Walsh, 2018). To effectively apply a decolonial lens in the analysis of life history data from Black people and people of African descent, researchers must center Black voices and acknowledge the impact of historical injustices in their analytical frameworks.

Afrocentric Life History Analysis

Within the tradition of Africana studies, this framework ensures that life history data are analyzed through African-centered values, communal knowledge systems, and a strengths-based approach. It incorporates prioritizing oral traditions and centering research participants' self-representation.

African and diasporic cultures value oral traditions as a means of preserving history, identity, and knowledge. Prioritizing oral traditions and storytelling demands researchers to treat stories as knowledge, not just as data. Researchers should approach stories as a valuable source of meaningful insight, wisdom, experiences, and perspectives that can provide a deeper understanding of a culture, community, or individual. Stories convey meaning, context, and perspective, allowing researchers to identify patterns and themes that may not be immediately apparent. Researchers should adopt a more critical and reflexive mindset, consider the social, cultural, and historical contexts in which stories are created and shared, and develop a more empathetic and understanding approach to research and analysis.

For example, a researcher studying the experiences of immigrants in a new country collects their stories and analyzes them, searching for patterns, themes, and deeper meanings that reveal the immigrants' experiences, values, and beliefs. This analysis also considers the social, cultural, and historical contexts in which the narratives were created and shared. For instance, when one immigrant states, "as a family, we struggled to meet our basic needs such as food and clothing," it does not necessarily mean that the family lacked the financial resources to purchase food or clothing. It could also indicate that they did not know where to find African stores that sold items specific to their culture. Prioritizing traditions in such a story requires the researcher to dig deeply into the values around food and clothing for that Black community. It also involves analyzing additional cultural and symbolic data such as proverbs, metaphors, music, and the storied meaning embedded in them.

It is therefore important to remember that Western thematic analysis frameworks may decontextualize Black life histories by over-relying on the researcher's reflections while disregarding the importance of involving reflections of the story owners. For example, if a participant describes their migration experience as "carrying my ancestors with me," you may want to interpret this not just as resilience but as an Afrocentric epistemological worldview of ancestral guidance and spiritual protection. Analyze such stories holistically rather than fragmenting them into disconnected themes. As much as possible, incorporate African-centered philosophies such as ubuntu (I am because we are) in themes about interconnectedness, sankofa (looking back to move forward) in themes about historical consciousness, and nommo (the power of the spoken word) for themes emphasizing verbal expression as empowerment.

Centering Research Participants' Self-Representation

Centering research participants' self-representation rather than external interpretations of their experiences, which can sometimes be inaccurate and incomplete, is an important aspect of decolonial Afrocentric analysis. Centering participants' self-representation promotes nuanced and accurate understandings of diverse experiences; doing so fosters empathy, respect, and empowerment. It is a Heshima practice. As a way of practicing Heshima in life history data analysis, being caring and respectful requires researchers to share their reflections with research participants and get their validation. Some Black scholars have applied similar techniques at different stages of data analysis.

- In a study about Black male teachers' recollections on the suffering of Black male youth, Pabon (2016) methodically transcribed and scrutinized interviews with close and repeated listening, constructed profiles from interview transcripts, returned profiles to participants for review, incorporated feedback from participants, then searched for common themes across participant profiles.
- In a study about shared experiences of Black women engineering students (Stitt & Happel-Parkins, 2019), the authors utilized a combination of intersectional and thematic analysis. The interviews were transcribed; terms that reflected Black feminist thought were recorded and used to develop initial codes. The initial codes were colorized, then used to identify similar experiences across participants. Each transcript was read and manually color-coded line by line using the initial coding. A secondary coding list was created to include phrases and terms that did not fit into the initial coding; codes for interviews were reviewed for "meaning units" (Stitt & Happel-Parkins, 2019, p. 67)—that is, phrases and sentences presenting ideas that should stand

alone. Some of the meaning units were overlapping or combined in some way. Study participants were asked for feedback after development of interview themes for member checking to include participant perspectives about how their interviews were analyzed; no changes were suggested by participants.

- Another example of data reflection that sought participant feedback is from a life history study that investigated cultural continuum of Black male pedagogy using a Black middle school teacher (Milton-Williams & Bryan, 2021). The study was informed by CRT, and the analysis took an interpretive manual coding approach. At least one day post-interview, the researchers listened to each interview with a fresh ear. The researchers took notes on follow-up questions. They engaged in multiple readings of transcripts, looking at keywords or potential relationships to discuss later. They shared notes among the research team and the study participant for more questions or perspectives. Based on the feedback, they considered the next interview topic before proceeding with the second and third interviews, and the process repeated after each interview. Data collection and analysis were overlapping phases in which researchers "attempted to bring his [the participant's] words to life on paper while recognizing and capturing the essence of what he said" (p. 45).

In the above examples, fostering participants' self-representation or seeking feedback during the analysis is an act of Heshima and should be done in analyzing life history data with Black people and people of African descent. Follow-up interviews where participants reflect on their own narratives are important for demonstrating not only prioritization of participants' stories in their own voices but also respect and care. Below are two examples of fictional study scenarios.

Fictional Example #1: Centering Black People's Self-Representation in Analyzing Life History Data

A researcher is conducting life history research on Black youth in the criminal justice system. Instead of relying solely on external interpretations or data collected by non-Black adults, they use participatory research methods by involving the youth in collecting and analyzing the stories. They facilitate the youth to take an active role in analyzing and interpreting the stories, using techniques such as co-coding, identifying themes, and co-interpretation to ensure that the youth's voices and perspectives are centered (Salami et al., 2021). Youth-led data analysis eliminates bias due to age-based power differences. The interpretation of data yields themes that are useful and relevant to Black youth rather than those that fit themes pre-determined by the researcher based on a literature review (Ejegi-Memeh et al., 2025).

Fictional Example #2: Use an Afrocentric Lens

If a Black participant describes being "spirit-led" in making life decisions, a Western lens might code this as intuition, while an Afrocentric lens respects it as a valid spiritual epistemology. You will not know this unless you engage in member checking and story circling. Self-representation can be incorporated at the individual participant level or at the Black community level.

To enhance Black community self-representation, researchers should engage in Afrocentric peer review. This might include inviting Black scholars, activists, or community leaders and members to critique the analysis and provide feedback. By fostering self-representation, the researcher can:

• Center the voices and perspectives of Black youth, providing a more nuanced and accurate understanding of their lives and experiences.

- Challenge dominant narratives and stereotypes about Black youth in the criminal justice system, providing a more nuanced and contextualized understanding of the issues from the vantage point of the youth.
- Facilitate Black youth in the criminal justice system to tell and take ownership of their stories and experiences, providing a platform for them to share their perspectives and advocate for the change they want.

Research participants' self-representation can be underpinned by the AOST framework (Osei, 2019, 2021) and Asante's (1980) Afrocentricity, both of which position Black people's culture, values, spirituality, communal resilience, ancestral wisdom, collective well-being, and experiences at the center rather than as deviations from Western norms and focusing solely on deficit narratives. This approach not only offers a more nuanced understanding but also honors the full humanity of Black individuals.

Strengths-Based and Joy-Centered Approaches

To truly capture the complexities and richness of Black experiences, researchers must center the strengths of Black communities. Some researchers only focus on historical trauma and deficit themes in the data and overlook Black experiences of resilience, joy, survival, creativity, agency, and Afrofuturism. While nuanced historical reflections are important, incorporating perspectives of Black people's present and future yields richer analysis. For instance, one of the strength- and joy-based approaches applicable to Africana studies is the Black joy and Afrofuturism approach to research (Keren, 2022; Reynaldo, 2016; Young-Scaggs, 2021) that is gaining popularity as a way to move beyond struggle narratives in life history research to focus on joy, innovation, and hope. For example, in a study analyzing the phenomenon of Black women's nude protest against violence in South Africa, where nakedness is associated with shame, the authors focus on the resourcefulness of using the naked body for future political intervention (Young, 2020b).

Life history researchers of Black communities can also code their stories for Black cultural practices such as music, fashion, and spirituality as spaces of community or individual liberation and satisfaction. Intentionally avoid deficit coding that, for example, extracts themes of pain, evil, crime, disease. Instead, look for codes and themes of Black joy, spirituality, humor, music, agency, community building, healing, and cultural pride. For instance, a Black woman narrating her experience of discrimination might recall not just the oppression but also how Black churches and jazz clubs were places of joy and resistance during times of precarity. Such themes should be fully explored and analyzed. If the researcher is not well grounded in ubuntu and does not practice Heshima in their RTA, they may fall short of using a strength-based lens in analyzing such a story.

Asset-based approaches recognize cultural wealth in Black communities (e.g., familial bonds, spirituality, activism). An example of a strength-based lens is provided by Yosso (2005), who challenged deficit thinking in education by developing the community cultural wellness model. Yosso advocates for research that focuses on marginalized communities' cultural knowledge, skills, abilities, and contacts. She identifies assets or cultural capital of college students of color. These include aspirational capital (ability to aspire for social mobility due to education despite the barriers), linguistic capital (ability to improve their communication skills), familial capital (preexisting personal and human resources), social capital (advantages of personal contacts), and navigational capital (ability to navigate institutional structures). Using an asset-based approach when thematizing Black life history data (e.g., in RTA), researchers can intentionally seek out expressions of strength, empowerment, and celebration, ensuring a balanced narrative.

Centering Intersectional Communal and Generational Knowledge

Black life histories are often not individualistic but deeply intertwined with family, ancestors, and collective experiences. Researchers in the field of Africana studies should intentionally analyze Black life stories, not just as personal journeys but as communal narratives. It is important to pay attention to intergenerational themes (e.g., resilience passed down, cultural traditions maintained). Codes and themes such as ancestral memory, or how participants invoke ancestors, past struggles, or historical continuity in their life experiences, should be intentionally captured. For example, a Black grandmother recalling her childhood in the Caribbean may describe not only her own experiences but also what her grandmother taught her. Such interwoven storytelling must be thematically searched for and honored in a way that captures the intersectionality of diverse participants' identities and statuses. Being inclusive in implementing intersectional analysis is key. For example, when coding themes in RTA, researchers can examine how Black participants describe experiences differently based on their gender, class, sexuality, ability, migration status, marital status, spatial location, age, and so on.

A Worked Example of Data Analysis

Topic: Black youth high school experiences

Purpose of the study: To understand the experiences of Black youth within schooling environments

Data: Life stories of five Black youth (aged 18–24) from [city name] who recently completed high school

Analytical framework: Heshima, an Afrocentric method of interpreting and honoring Black life narratives. The framework borrows the concept of reflexivity from Braun and Clarke's (2019) RTA, which is coupled with co-reflexivity of research participants.

Excerpt of the story: (this example uses fictional data for illustrative purposes only)

Ayana, 19, University Student

Interviewer: Can you tell me about your experience in high school?

Ayana: High school was . . . complicated. I did well in my classes, but I always felt like I was being watched. Like people were expecting me to fail. My grade 9 teacher told me I was too loud. I stopped talking after that. But inside I was still screaming. I used to raise my hand all the time in middle school, but after that comment, I kind of disappeared in the classroom. I didn't want to be the "problem." I just wanted to get through without drawing attention. I had to learn to breathe shallow, to take up less space.

{learning while invisible; breathing}

[silence]

Ayana: It made me question everything about myself. Was I being *too much*? Too visible? I started shrinking. And yet, I still felt like I was under a microscope. Like being quiet didn't protect me either. I felt like there was no right way to be me in that space. I just had to keep watch over myself.

{schooling with an open eye}

[silence]

Interviewer: Did anyone see you differently?

Ayana: Ms. Thompson. She was the only Black teacher we had. She *saw* me. Not in a performative way but really saw me. She'd pull me aside and just say, *"You okay, baby?"* I can't explain how much that meant. Just hearing someone speak to me like that—with warmth, with care—it grounded me. She made school feel a warmer place for me.

{resistance as a way of breathing; community support}

[smiles]

Interviewer: Were there any positive moments during that time?

Ayana: Starting the Black Student Alliance changed everything for me. It gave me a place to breathe. At first, it was just three of us meeting in a hallway during lunch. By the end of the year, we had events, speakers, even a poetry night. But even then, we got pushback. Admin told us not to make it "too political." That stung. Because my Blackness isn't a debate. It's just who I am.

{resistance as a way of breathing}

[silence]

Interviewer: Did you feel supported outside of school?

Ayana: My grandmother carried me through. She'd say, *"You come from strength, baby girl. Don't ever forget."* When things got hard, I'd close my eyes and imagine her hands on my shoulders. I'd walk through those school hallways like she was walking with me. That image gave me strength. That's how I survived.

{Ancestral and spiritual guidance through modern struggles; becoming the mirror}

[silence]

Interviewer: And now, what does success mean to you?

Ayana: Success is showing up whole. It's being able to speak again—not just out loud, but in ways that honour the parts of me that were silenced. It's refusing to shrink permanently. It's knowing that my voice matters—not in spite of being Black, but because of it.

{Afrofuturism}

Step 1: Read and reread the transcript to familiarize yourself with the data per Braun and Clarke's (2019) RTA.

Step 2: Generate codes: After reading and reading the story, in this example, I color-coded the transcript.

- The text in red highlights negative experiences.
- The green text highlights positive codes and experiences.
- The pink text represents community support.

Step 3: Generating themes. This step combines RTA's phases 3 and 4.

Based on the color codes, I thought through the potential themes that could be identified from the negative, positive, and community codes. I chose to overlook the negative themes and focus on the positive and community-focused themes, and I listed them.

Step 4: Naming and defining themes.

The following are some of the themes identified from this exemplar data set and how I named them:

- Learning while invisible—stories of exclusion masked as neutrality.
- Schooling with one eye open—hypervigilance in white-dominant spaces.
- Resistance as a way of breathing—daily acts of asserting one's voice.
- Ancestral and spiritual guidance through modern struggles—holding cultural strength amid systemic pushbacks.
- Becoming the mirror—moments when they saw themselves reflected and loved.
- Afrofuturism—having a vision of the future amidst the precarity.

Table 4.1 shows the researcher's interpretations of the data. Now that you have your themes, reflections, and their implications in a matrix format, and this is the time to check your interpretation with the participants to ensure that your interpretation of

Table 4.1 Summary of Emerging Themes

Theme	Quote	Researcher's reflection	Implications	Remarks
Learning while invisible	My grade 9 teacher told me I was too loud. I stopped talking after that. But inside I was still screaming.	This line speaks directly to the violence of invisible exclusion. The student is physically present but emotionally silenced, and that silence is internalized. The participant's silence can be interpreted as resistance.	Schools should center cultural humility and value human diversity—not every student can speak in a uniform tone. The ministry of education should dismantle the myth of neutrality in classroom practices that exclude students who do not conform to white classroom norms.	This theme speaks to the state of constant alertness, self-monitoring, and guardedness some Black students may experience in educational institutions shaped by whiteness.
	I just wanted to get through without drawing attention.	Ayana's quiet agency is a response to the violence of invisible exclusion. Surviving the attention provides the peace she needs to get through the day.	Researchers should value silence as a form of knowledge.	
Schooling with one eye open	I just had to keep watch over myself.	Even while learning, this participant must remain on guard. She experienced daily aggression in the form of surveillance. She learned to read with one eye while using the other to keep guard.	Acknowledge the racialized emotional labor of Black learners. Create spaces where Blackness is not only accepted but centered and affirmed. Decolonize pedagogical practices that demand conformity and erasure of Black norms. Educators should recognize and challenge their own biases and the surveillance culture embedded in schools.	This theme deeply aligns with the Heshima framework, which centers respect, recognition, and restoration in the research process. It urges us to look beyond what is spoken and examine the tensions in what is withheld or masked—out of necessity for self-preservation.

Theme	Quote	Researcher's reflection	Implications	Remarks
Resistance as a way of breathing	Starting the Black Student Alliance changed everything for me. It gave me a place to breathe... I had to learn to breathe shallow, to take up less space.	In the first quote, breathing symbolizes safety—a sanctuary in an oppressive context, a reclamation of dignity. The second quote reveals agency in embodied vigilance, where breath becomes both a battleground and a compass for navigating safety and survival.	Educational settings should provide Black-led student spaces, not just as symbolic gestures but as spaces for emotional and cultural oxygen. Institutions should move beyond traditional metrics of inclusion and ensure that Black students can feel like they can breathe and belong.	The theme challenges the idea that resistance must be loud, visible, or articulate. In the Heshima framework, such experiences reflect the invisible labor where Black people must navigate the tension between being seen and being safe.
Ancestral and spiritual guidance	When things got hard, I'd close my eyes and imagine her hands on my shoulders. I'd walk through those school hallways like she was walking with me. That image gave me strength. That's how I survived.	This theme acknowledges knowledge passed down through stories, proverbs, songs, names, and silences—as valid and vital epistemology. Respect and honoring intergenerational wisdom and Afrocentric forms of knowledge and resistance.	This theme speaks to the ongoing presence and influence of ancestors in the lives of Black people—not only as memory or legacy, but as active, guiding forces. It recognizes that spiritual knowledge and ancestral connection shape how many Black individuals interpret their experiences, make decisions, and navigate both struggle and hope.	In Afrocentric research, this is a key part of epistemic respect—researchers should value ways of knowing that do not always fit Western paradigms.
Becoming the mirror	My grandmother carried me through. She'd say, "You come from strength, baby girl. Don't ever forget."	In this relationship, the grandmother reflects strength back to the participant, teaching her to see herself as powerful and resilient. She is encouraged to integrate her grandmother's strength into her own understanding of herself, thus mirroring that power back into the world through her actions, choices, and presence.	Black people and people of African descent are interconnected. This participant's story is also a story of her grandmother, and both should be honored and respected.	Heshima scholars could collect oral histories, exploring how stories, proverbs, and wisdom from elders shape and sustain identity formation.
Afrofuturism	Success is showing up whole...	Black identity is reclaimed as a source of vision, strength, and future building.	This theme is about reimagining what it means to be fully alive, Black, and free in the world to come.	This theme suggests that creating a future where marginalized communities are respected is possible through the refusal to accept erasure.

their story aligns with theirs. Milton-Williams and Bryan (2022), Pabon (2016), and Stitt and Happel-Parkins (2019) are examples of researchers who have sought or incorporated Black community participants' feedback in their analyses. Again, following their examples, before writing up your findings, researchers should return to participants or their community and confirm their interpretations.

Step 5: Reporting

The rest of the writing follows the identified themes and how they fit into the purpose of the study. For this exemplar study, the purpose was to understand the experiences of Black youth within schooling environments. I would present the findings in the same order in which the themes were defined. While writing the report, it is important to ensure that the findings benefit Black communities rather than just academic discourse. To achieve this, researchers must actively decolonize their mind and engage in asking questions to themselves such as the following:

- What do these findings contribute to existing literature on the topic?
- How do these findings inform or disrupt existing oppressive systems and anti-Blackness?
- What do the results mean to diverse categories of Black people and people of African descent?
- What are the implications of these findings for future research, policy, and practice?

CHAPTER SUMMARY

In this chapter, I noted that the researcher's reflections and interpretations, however thoughtful, are not enough. I offered Heshima as an analytical framework encompassing approaches that center Black epistemologies, voices, experiences, perspectives, and cultures in research. Decolonial and Afrocentric analysis, which prioritizes oral traditions rooted in philosophies such as Ubuntu, Sankofa, and Nommo, should be utilized. Additionally, frameworks that center research participants' self-representation should be prioritized. Centering research participants' self-representation means engaging them in co-coding and co-interpreting data. Such frameworks include the strength-based and joy-centered approaches in which researchers intentionally code for strength, empowerment, and celebration instead of pain, crime, evil, and other negative aspects of human life. Another approach is characterized by centering intersectional communal and generational knowledge. Black life histories are often not individualistic but deeply intertwined with family, ancestors, collective experiences, and the intersectionality of identities and statuses. I provided a worked example of analysis of an interview transcript based on steps adapted from Braun and Clarke's (2019) RTA.

FURTHER READING

McClish-Boyd, K., & Bhattacharya, K. (2024). Methodological Considerations for endarkened narrative inquiry. *Qualitative Inquiry*, *30*(7), 584–594. https://doi.org/10.1177/10778004231186565

CHAPTER 5
Knowledge Mobilization

INTRODUCTION

This chapter covers how to share research findings with relevant audiences to ensure that they are useful to the Black people and people of African descent who participated in the study. It covers how to communicate your findings in a transparent, efficient, accessible, and ethical process. How can one distinguish between what and what not—to disseminate and translate?

Knowledge mobilization is the process of making research knowledge accessible, usable, and impactful beyond academic settings through strengthening relationships between researchers and knowledge users, including communities, policymakers, and educators (Levin, 2013). It involves sharing, exchanging, and applying knowledge in ways that inform practice, influence policy, support communities, and create meaningful social change. Knowledge mobilization is a multifaceted process that involves several core components. Dissemination is a critical aspect, where research findings are shared through various channels such as reports, presentations, and digital platforms. However, dissemination is only one part of the equation. Effective knowledge mobilization also requires engagement.

Furthermore, knowledge mobilization should prioritize exchange, valuing two-way conversations where knowledge flows both from and to communities, rather than being a one-way transmission. Knowledge mobilization matters because only "to know is not enough" (Levin, 2013, p. 2).

Decolonial Black Knowledge Mobilization

In working with Black people and people of African descent, it is important to decolonize knowledge mobilization. Decolonial knowledge mobilization refers to the intentional process of sharing and activating knowledge in ways that challenge colonial power structures, center historically marginalized voices, and honor community-rooted ways of knowing. Not all knowledge mobilization strategies yield positive results. In fact, some can reinforce negative stereotypes and harm as unintended consequences of research (L. T. Smith, 2020). In the context of life history research with Black people, decolonial mobilization is essential because it resists extractive research practices and instead prioritizes relational accountability, cultural relevance, and community empowerment. By mobilizing knowledge through culturally grounded and accessible platforms—like storytelling, art, oral traditions, and digital media—researchers ensure that Black life histories are not only preserved but also used to spark dialogue, policy change, healing, and intergenerational learning.

Decolonial strategies for Black knowledge mobilization prioritize the perspectives, values, and experiences of Black people and people of African descent in the dissemination and application of knowledge. These strategies aim to center Black voices, epistemologies, and cultural practices in the process of sharing and utilizing knowledge, rather than relying on dominant Western frameworks. They are community-led strategies that involve partnering with Black community organizations, leaders, and knowledge holders to co-share research meaningfully with stakeholders. This approach ensures that research is shared in contextualized ways relevant to the study communities. Centering community voices and expertise can facilitate the translation of research into tangible outcomes that support the well-being and self-determination of Black communities. This collaborative approach helps to shift the power dynamics in research, positioning Black communities as leaders and drivers of knowledge dissemination and application.

Components of Decolonial Black Knowledge Mobilization

a. *Codesigning dissemination plans*

Involve community partners from the outset to collaboratively decide:

- The findings that should be shared—not all findings can be shared with everyone. Some Black stories might have included information that is not for public consumption. Researchers need to be aware of and respect the cultural and community protocols regarding the sharing of traditional Black community knowledge. This includes maintaining confidentiality and anonymity to protect the interests of participants. Certain research findings, especially those related to traditional knowledge of or strategies for navigating systemic oppression, may need to remain undisclosed. Sharing this information publicly could jeopardize the safety and effectiveness of these strategies. Such sacred knowledge can be identified and removed from publicly shareable knowledge at the outset. Formation of community advisory boards is key at the inception of the project. The community advisory boards can provide oversight on what is shared and how, ensuring cultural respect and accountability.
- How information should be communicated, for example, in meetings, written materials or digital resources. Target

audiences/community members should lead the researcher in identifying relevant stakeholders for sharing research results.

b. *Use of culturally relevant dissemination channels*

Research results can be shared with members of the Black communities using channels that are "relevant" and comfortable for them, such as Black community meetings, which might include the following:

- kitchen table conversations—that is, informal, conversational, and often small-group discussions or interviews, typically held in a comfortable and familiar environment (Farrell Racette, 2022).
- "meeting at this tree" (Toliver et al., 2019, p. 45)—a gathering under a metaphorical tree where marginalized voices and identities can be amplified and heard, in contrast to traditional townhalls[1] where they might be overlooked or silenced. A tree can be a real or an imaginary one, such as a place in a park or at the beach.
- faith-based or spirituality-based gatherings—these meetings can be particularly beneficial for disseminating research within Black communities. They integrate spiritual principles and values with academic and scientific research, fostering a deeper understanding of and holistic approach to research findings.

---

[1]The traditional town hall model has been criticized for its roots in settler colonialism, where settlers established towns to exert control over land and community members and gathered to exercise democratic power over a geographic space that had been forcibly taken from Indigenous peoples, perpetuating colonization (Toliver et al., 2019).

- Black barbershop talks—informal gatherings of Black men at a local barbershop where research findings can be shared and discussed in a relaxed, familiar, and comfortable setting. Barbershop conversations can spark insightful responses to the research findings and generate diverse perspectives and recommendations.

c. *Reflexivity and positionality*

It is essential for researchers to be transparent about their social location and to recognize the power dynamics at play. By embracing humility and respect during the knowledge mobilization phase, you can foster a more inclusive and impactful process.

d. *Feedback loops*

Use member checking and validation sessions to confirm interpretations with community members. Allow communities to challenge or refine what data are being represented, and how.

e. *Coauthorship with community members*

Euro-Western ideas of knowledge mobilization often influence how research is shared through traditional academic articles. However, it is possible to disseminate research through scholarly articles in ways that respect and honor the contributions of Black participants and knowledge users. One effective strategy is to invite community partners to coauthor academic and public-facing materials. This method ensures that the work is grounded in Black perspectives and experiences, truly reflecting authentic voices. Coauthorship can extend to various types of publications, including newspapers, newsletters, infographics, and evidence briefs. Researchers should also aim to publish in Black and African studies journals where their content is less likely to face censorship from non-Black reviewers.

CASE STUDY: THE KITCHEN TABLE CONVERSATION

A kitchen table conversation is a casual meeting that can take place in an informal place such as someone's kitchen or backyard, a local café, or in a "fireside" (Osei-Tutu, 2021a) space. Although a kitchen can be understood as a patriarchal, gendered space, it can also be perceived as a space where human connections are strengthened, serving as a venue for empowerment and liberation (Kohl & McCutcheon, 2015). It is a space where women have the power to make decisions, even in patriarchal societies. In a regular family setting, the kitchen table is where people share food, drinks, laughter, and everyday stories that deepen their connections. The kitchen serves as an excellent space to share research results on Black life history, seek permission for wider dissemination, and reach agreements with the community on the best methods to do so. Kitchen tables have been used in community social political movements (Voices for Indi, 2023) as well as in academic research. They have been utilized in arts-based Indigenous research (e.g., Farrell Racette, 2022) and as a data collection method in qualitative research projects (e.g., Harb et al., 2024; Navarro et al., 2013). However, they are also applicable to Africana studies for mobilizing knowledge about Black and other marginalized and diasporic communities. The relaxed informal environment of the kitchen table conversation facilitates dialogue and safety for Black folks to engage with the research findings and meaningfully deliberate on how to use them for their benefit. It is a space protected from unwanted intrusion and oppressive noise. The kitchen table can therefore provide Black communities with the intimacy and safety required for open dialogue about issues of concern (Williams, 2017). According to Williams (2017, p. 980), "it is only from the confines of our kitchen tables that we can stop outsiders from interrupting our conversations about freedom, about our politics, about our struggle, and about how we educate our children." Unlike standard academic conferences that often involve peers who may not understand your research participants' life experiences, the kitchen table serves as more than just a platform for presenting findings. It is a space for engaging with community members to collaboratively envision necessary changes to the current situation. This approach allows for a break from the dominant, often unempathetic, academic protocols of the Euro-Western tradition. Additionally, kitchen tables can be an effective strategy for enhancing communication between researchers and Black practitioners in the field of your topic.

Exemplar kitchen table plan for life history research with Black people and people of African descent

This is a kitchen table plan for disseminating life history research using the kitchen table approach. This method centers dignity, relational accountability, ancestral wisdom, and collective meaning making within Black communities (Figure 5.1).

Guiding values from the Heshima framework:

- *Dignity and respect:* All stories are sacred and must be treated with care. Share the findings with sensitivity and compassion, representing stories in a respectful and accurate manner and prioritizing confidentiality, anonymity, and consent.
- *Ethical relationality:* Knowledge is co-held and shaped in dialogue; therefore, engaging participants and their communities is key.
- *Memory, legacy, and spirituality:* When disseminating life history research with Black people and people of African descent, consider the cultural significance of storytelling and its connection to memory, legacy, and spirituality. A culturally sensitive and respectful approach prioritizes respectful representation, community engagement, and spiritual and emotional care, acknowledging the historical and ongoing struggles of Black communities and the role of spirituality in their survival.

- *Voice and validation:* Participants define meaning and significance. Always remember to hold space for participants to
  respond to the information being provided.

Step 1: Build Community Relationships

Relationship building for knowledge mobilization should be an
integral part of the research process, which begins at the project's inception. To effectively disseminate knowledge within a
community, it is important to involve respected community leaders and stakeholders with study participants in predissemination
conversations. These discussions should focus on the group's
preferences for receiving information. Provide some written
material for them to read prior to the meeting. Establishing
trust, actively listening to their concerns, and demonstrating a
genuine interest in their needs and perspectives are critical for
achieving success.

Step 2: Codesign the Kitchen Table Space

In collaboration with community members and study participants, choose a familiar, comfortable, accessible, and welcoming
location. Aim to cocreate an environment that allows participants to incorporate culturally affirming elements that reflect
Black traditions, such as candles, fabrics, food, music, or art. This
will foster a sense of belonging, community, and connection.

Step 3: Frame the Setting

- Begin with land acknowledgment or prayer led by a local
  elder or spiritual leader as an opening ritual.
- Briefly explain the purpose of the research and the event,
  honoring participants and ancestors whose stories inform
  the findings.
- Frame the gathering as a mutual knowledge exchange, not an
  academic presentation. Shift the emphasis from a top-down

approach, where the researcher presents information to an audience, to a collaborative environment where all participants share their insights and experiences. This approach fosters a sense of community and encourages open dialogue, making everyone feel valued and engaged. By validating your themes with individual participants beforehand, you would have created a foundation of trust and respect. This prior engagement allows you to enter the gathering with a clear understanding of the perspectives and knowledge each person brings to the table. The goal is to create an atmosphere where participants feel comfortable expressing their opinions and where the collective wisdom can emerge organically. Researchers must remain flexible and humble, recognizing that each kitchen table gathering will be shaped by the specific community's rhythms, needs, and ancestral ways of knowing.

Figure 5.1   Kitchen table illustration

Source: Author.

Note: These are not real people. The image was created for illustrative purposes using Adobe, 2025.

Step 4: Engage in Dialogue and Co-reflection

Share selected life history data using agreed-upon methods such as storytelling and multimedia. If you must share participants' quotes, integrate them with respect and dignity, using their own words and language. Take regular pauses for reflection and invite attendees to share what the stories evoke for them and what truths they perceive. You can use open-ended questions such as the following:

• What resonates with your own experience?
• What do these stories tell us about our future?
• What do we want to do with this knowledge?

In other words, instead of dominating the conversation with a formal presentation, you can invite participants to share their thoughts on the analysis, encouraging them to build on it, critique it, or offer alternative viewpoints.

Encouraging participants to guide the process not only enhances the richness of the discussion but also empowers them to take ownership of the knowledge being created. This can lead to innovative ideas and solutions that might not emerge in a traditional presentation format. Ultimately, viewing the gathering as a collaborative exchange helps to strengthen relationships, deepen understanding, and foster a culture of continuous learning among all involved. The researcher or a selected community member can facilitate the dialogue based on the arrangement with the stakeholders. For example, you can introduce one topic at a time and go around the table giving people an opportunity to contribute. Honor silence as a valid contribution and open the conversation until everyone is happy to move to the next topic.

Step 5: Ground the Knowledge in Action

After gathering insights and perspectives, ask the group questions to encourage final collective recommendations or visions for change, such as "Who else should be hearing about this research?" To build momentum, invite participants to participate or take on leadership roles in implementing the next steps. These could include creating community zines, engaging other stakeholders such as practitioners, policy implementers, or other research audiences, and generating new ideas for future research. This process promotes meaningful action and positive change.

Step 6: Reciprocity and Closure

Among Black people and people of African descent, the act of sharing food is a ritual that embodies a deep cultural significance. Food serves as a bridge, fostering connections and nurturing a sense of community. Hosting a kitchen table conversation requires thoughtful consideration of what to serve, as traditional dishes can evoke shared histories and celebrate cultural heritage. Providing attendees with the opportunity to share not only food and drinks but also honoraria "promotes" inclusivity and respect. Additionally, offering printed or digital materials such as brochures, handouts, or digital links ensures that participants leave with knowledge and a tangible reminder of the conversations. These materials can contain information about community resources, local initiatives, or educational content that may encourage further engagement and networking. Conclude the conversation with expressions of gratitude, affirmations, and a commitment to maintaining relationships.

The kitchen table format can be followed to organize and conduct other small dissemination meetings, such as a "meeting at this tree," a Black barbershop talk, or a faith-based gathering.

DIGITAL PLATFORMS

In the digital age, the dissemination of research findings has expanded beyond traditional academic channels to include innovative, accessible, and interactive digital platforms. Tools such as

ArcGIS StoryMaps (Dangermond & Dangermond, 1969) and Omeka (Roy Rosenzweig Center for History and New Media and the Corporation for Digital Scholarship & George Mason University, 2008) have emerged as powerful means for scholars to present research in ways that are visually engaging, community responsive, and publicly accessible. These platforms offer researchers the opportunity to curate narratives, artifacts, and geographic data in formats that are not only informative but also immersive, which bridges the gap between academic knowledge and public engagement. The sections below describe the use of ArcGIS StoryMaps and Omeka in disseminating life history research, particularly within and about Black communities, and highlight their potential to honor lived experiences, foster dialogue, and democratize knowledge sharing beyond the walls of the academy.

ArcGIS StoryMaps

ArcGIS StoryMaps is a platform that is a product of the Environmental Systems Research Institute, or Esri (Dangermond & Dangermond, 1969). Jack and Laura Dangermond cofounded Esri to use technology to balance human development and environmental stewardship. They drew inspiration from their work at Harvard's laboratory for computer graphics and spatial analysis, where early mapmaking software was developed. Esri initially focused on environmental studies for land-use planning projects. Through continuous innovation, research, and development and a customer-centric approach, Esri became the world leader in geographic information system (GIS) software, now widely used across various sectors.

StoryMaps (short for ArcGIS StoryMaps) evolved from Esri's desire to combine the power of GIS with engaging narrative storytelling. The concept took shape around 2012 when Esri recognized the potential to make maps more accessible and understandable to a broader audience. The idea was to create a platform that allowed users to integrate maps with text, images, and multimedia in a cohesive and interactive way. By leveraging their existing mapping technology, Esri developed StoryMaps to allow users to create compelling visual narratives that effectively communicate information about specific locations or themes. Over the years, story maps have become popular in various fields, including education, journalism, conservation, and public engagement. Examples about Black communities include New York City Landmarks Preservation Commission (2025), University of South Florida (2022), and WE ACT (2024). The Black Towns and Settlements Project also used StoryMaps to present existing and historical Black towns and settlements in North America (Davis, 2022).

A story map typically integrates various forms of media—such as maps, images, charts, and text—into a single cohesive narrative. This format is particularly helpful in showcasing geographical data and environmental studies, as it allows researchers to illustrate their findings spatially while guiding the audience through the research process. By blending visuals with storytelling, researchers can distill complex datasets into digestible insights. This approach not only increases understanding but also fosters a deeper connection to the research, encouraging audiences to engage with the findings.

Additionally, story maps can be easily shared online, making them a powerful tool for widespread dissemination that can be accessed from anywhere, promoting greater public awareness and discourse around important issues. By incorporating story maps into research, data dissemination strategies can significantly improve the way findings are shared and understood. By utilizing this technique, researchers can present their life history research findings in a manner that is both informative and engaging, paving the way for more effective communication and collaboration in the scientific community.

Why Apply ArcGIS StoryMaps to Black Life History Research?

Using the StoryMaps platform to disseminate Black life history data has several advantages:

- *Honoring place in Black life histories:* For many Black communities, place—whether ancestral homelands, neighborhoods, places for practicing faith and spirituality, or migration routes—is deeply tied to identity, memory, and resilience. The StoryMaps platform offers a powerful tool for visualizing and sharing the complex narratives of Black experiences. By embedding maps that show migration pathways, resettlement stories, or historical landmarks such as former Black townships and cultural hubs, researchers can create a rich and immersive storytelling experience. These maps can be further enhanced with photographs, oral history clips, or quotes tied to specific geographic points, providing a nuanced and multifaceted understanding of the past. Additionally, layered maps can be used to illustrate the dynamics of displacement, resistance, and community organizing over time, offering a compelling and interactive way to explore the complexities of Black history and culture.

- *Elevating voice through multimedia narratives:* StoryMaps can be used to elevate Black community voice through multimedia narratives. Life history research relies on rich personal stories, and StoryMaps lets these stories come alive through voice, image, and interaction. For example, the researcher can embed audio recordings of community leaders or members reflecting on pivotal life moments. You can include visual art, poetry, or spoken word created by participants.

- *Connecting the past, present, and future:* Afrofuturist and Afrocentric approaches to life history research emphasize the interconnectedness of past, present, and future, highlighting the ways in which nonlinear time shapes our understanding of the world. This perspective is crucial for understanding the complexities and experiences of Black people and people of African descent. It acknowledges the ongoing impacts of colonial and postcolonial disruptions on contemporary life. By using the StoryMaps platform, researchers can create interactive timelines that move from historical events to current-day activism and future aspirations, providing a dynamic and immersive experience. Embedded videos, digital art, and other multimedia elements created by participants can be used to highlight community aspirations, offering a powerful way to visualize the connections between past, present, and future.

- *Community-led cocreation and control:* Community-led cocreation and control are essential for ensuring that dissemination is not extractive but rather a collaborative process that empowers communities to shape and coauthor their own stories. By involving community members in the curation and creation of content, such as submitting photographs, quotes, and stories, researchers can ensure that the narratives are authentic and meaningful. Furthermore, storing the project on a community-owned platform or server guarantees data sovereignty, allowing communities to maintain control over their own data. By providing editing access or workshop time for youth and elders to shape the content together, researchers can facilitate intergenerational collaboration and knowledge sharing, ultimately producing a more nuanced and accurate representation of Black community stories.

- *Public education and policy influence:* Life history research has the potential to inform education, advocacy, and system transformation, but only if shared in an accessible and impactful way. The StoryMaps platform is a powerful tool

for achieving this goal, enabling researchers to create interactive community exhibits that can be projected at town
halls, schools, or libraries, bringing the stories and experiences of communities to life. By including a section with
calls to action or community-generated recommendations,
researchers can empower audiences to take action and
become involved in creating positive change. Furthermore,
sharing the map with policy stakeholders or funders can
amplify the voices and stories of Black communities, providing a compelling visual representation of the impact of
systemic issues and the need for transformative solutions.

Utilizing multimedia narratives such as story maps is an effective
way to elevate the voices of Black communities and ensure their
stories are authentically represented.

Omeka

Omeka is a tool that helps people create and share digital collections online. Imagine that you as a researcher have collected a
bunch of artifacts including objects, images, documents, and
videos that tell a story about Black people or people of African
descent as individuals, families, or communities. You can then
digitize these and use Omeka to tell the stories embedded in the
items. Omeka allows you to organize the items in a way that
makes it easy for others to explore and learn from them.

Omeka is a user-friendly platform that does not require technical
expertise, thanks to its simple and intuitive interface that makes
it accessible to everyone. One of its key strengths is its multimedia capabilities, which allow users to upload and display a wide
range of content, including text, images, audio, and video, creating rich, engaging presentations that bring stories to life.
Additionally, Omeka is highly customizable, offering flexibility
in organizing content and adding features that enhance the user

experience. As an open-source platform, Omeka is free to use and can be modified by anyone, making it an ideal solution for users with unique requirements who want to tailor the platform to their specific needs. Omeka is an excellent tool for disseminating the findings of life history research with Black people. Its open-source nature allows for customization and flexibility, enabling researchers to tailor their presentations to the specific needs and preferences of their audience. Omeka's multimedia capabilities, including the integration of text, images, audio, and video, provide a rich and engaging platform for sharing personal narratives and historical contexts. This is particularly important for life history research, as it allows for the authentic representation of individual experiences and community histories. Additionally, Omeka's user-friendly interface and accessibility features ensure that the research findings are easily accessible to a wide audience, fostering greater understanding and appreciation of the lived experiences of Black people. By using Omeka, researchers can create dynamic interactive presentations that not only inform but also inspire and empower the community.

Why Apply Omeka to Black Life History Research?

The Omeka exhibition platform brings various advantages to Black life history research:

- *Digital archiving of oral histories and artifacts:* Omeka provides a robust platform for the digital archiving of oral histories and artifacts, enabling the storage and presentation of a wide range of digitized materials. These can include audio and video interviews, photographs, letters, and documents, as well as artwork or personal mementos, all of which can be uploaded as individual items with detailed metadata. This metadata provides contextual information about each participant's story, making the materials easily

searchable and accessible and allowing for a rich and
nuanced understanding of the histories and experiences
being preserved.

- *Storytelling through thematic exhibits:* Life history researchers can use Omeka to craft compelling narratives by
organizing life history data into thematic exhibits that
explore topics such as Black migration, education, resistance, and spirituality. Each exhibit page can be designed to
provide an immersive experience, incorporating multimedia
elements, quotes, and in-depth analysis that offer visitors a
nuanced and layered understanding of participants' experiences. By curating content in this way, life history researchers
can create engaging and informative exhibits that bring the
stories and experiences of individuals to life, facilitating a
deeper understanding of the complex themes and issues that
shape their lives.

- *Collaborative and community-led curation:* Omeka facilitates collaborative curation, enabling community members
to play an active role in selecting materials to include in
exhibits. Participants can also contribute their own perspectives and insights, providing captions, titles, or reflective
pieces that offer a personal and nuanced understanding of
their stories. Furthermore, Omeka's collaborative approach
allows for intergenerational digital storytelling, where elders
and youth can work together to create meaningful and culturally grounded narratives rooted in Afrocentric frameworks
like Heshima that prioritize community-centered and
respectful approaches to storytelling.

- *Embedding cultural frameworks:* Researchers can embed
Black philosophies such as ubuntu, sankofa, and nommo and
ethical frameworks such as Heshima into the design of the
digital archive. This helps ensure that the platform reflects
and honors the cultural values and traditions of the communities it represents. This can be achieved by customizing

categories, tags, and metadata fields to incorporate culturally relevant values such as respect, healing, and memory. Additionally, researchers can include introductions or welcome pages in African descendant languages or dialects, adding a layer of cultural authenticity and accessibility. By incorporating aesthetics rooted in Black cultural design, the digital archive can become a vibrant and meaningful space that celebrates the richness and diversity of Black cultures.

- *Increasing accessibility and public engagement:* Omeka websites can significantly increase accessibility and public engagement by being open access, allowing community members, students, and the broader public to freely engage with the content. This openness enables the platform to serve as an educational tool in schools or community centers, providing a valuable resource for learning and exploration. Furthermore, Omeka websites are designed to be mobile responsive and easy to navigate, making them accessible to individuals with varying levels of comfort with using technology and ensuring that the content can be easily consumed and understood by a wide range of audiences.

Examples of projects involving Black people and people of African descent that have used the Omeka exhibit platform include the following:

- the September 11 digital archive (Roy Rosenzweig Center for History and New Media and the Corporation for Digital Scholarship, 2002)
- a student project that explored slavery stories among Black communities in small towns in the eastern seaboard (Counts, 2024)
- Hurricane Katrina and Rita digital memory bank (Roy Rosenzweig Center for History and New Media & University of New Orleans, 2005).

In conclusion, Omeka stands out as a powerful and versatile tool for disseminating the findings of life history research with Black people.

CHAPTER SUMMARY

In this chapter, I introduced you to strategies for mobilizing knowledge from life history research with Black people and people of African descent from a decolonial perspective. Decolonial Black knowledge mobilization requires careful consideration of several key factors, including codesigning dissemination plans with Black communities and stakeholders, utilizing culturally relevant dissemination channels such as the kitchen table conversation, meeting at this tree, and barbershop talks. I offered an example of how a kitchen table conversation can be planned and implemented. In addition to such strategies, it is also important to practice reflexivity and positionality to acknowledge the biases and privileges of researchers and practitioners. Additionally, establishing feedback loops to ensure ongoing dialogue and learning, and engaging in coauthorship with community members, researchers, and practitioners are crucial for promoting equitable and effective knowledge mobilization. By prioritizing these approaches, knowledge mobilization efforts can be more responsive to community needs and concerns and can promote social justice and equity for Black communities.

In this chapter, I also described how life history data can be mobilized through digital platforms such as ArcGIS StoryMaps and Omeka. These are only two examples of digital tools that are perfect for sharing items such as artifacts, photographs, as well as migration routes and landmarks in personal and community stories into a single digital narrative. While these are not the only strategies for mobilizing Black life history research knowledge, the chapter has focused on methods that depart from traditional Western ways.

References

Adams, T. E., Ellis, C., & Jones, S. H. (2017). Autoethnography. In J. Matthes, C. S. Davis, & R. F. Potter (Eds.), *The international encyclopedia of communication research methods* (1st ed., pp. 1–11). Wiley. https://doi.org/10.1002/9781118901731.iecrm0011

Akuoko-Barfi, C., Escobar Olivo, V., Rampersaud, M., Parada, H., & Shuster, R. (2025). "I feel like I was targeted": Black youth navigating policing in Ontario, Canada. *Child & Youth Services*, 46(1), 103–128. https://doi.org/10.1080/0145935X.2023.2243436

Antikainen, A. (2016). Introduction: In search of life history. In I. Goodson, A. Antikainen, P. Sikes, & M. Andrews (Eds.) *The Routledge international handbook on narrative and life history* (1st ed., pp. 131–143). Routledge. https://doi.org/10.4324/9781315768199

Asante, M. K. (1991). The Afrocentric idea in education. *The Journal of Negro Education*, 60(2), 170–180. https://doi.org/10.2307/2295608

Asante, M. (1998). *The Afrocentric idea* (Revised). Temple University Press. http://www.jstor.org/stable/j.ctt1bw1kjr

Asante, M. (2004). The Afrocentric idea. In R. L. Jackson II (Ed.), *African American communications and identities: Essential readings* (pp. 16–28). Sage Publications Ltd.

Asante, M. K. (2018). *The history of Africa: The quest for eternal harmony* (3rd ed.). Routledge. https://doi.org/10.4324/9781315168166

Asante, M. K. (2020). Afrocentricity. In *Routledge Handbook of pan-Africanism* (1st ed., pp. 147–158). Routledge. https://doi.org/10.4324/9780429020193

Awidi, M., & Al Hadidi, S. (2021). Participation of Black Americans in cancer clinical trials: Current challenges and proposed solutions. *JCO Oncology Practice*, 17(5), 265–271.

Beoku-Betts, J. (1994). When Black is not enough: Doing field research among Gullah women. *NWSA Journal, 6*(3), 413–433.

Best, A. L. (2022). Anti-black racism and power: Centering black scholars to achieve health equity. *Hastings Center Report, 52*(S1), S39–S41. https://doi.org/10.1002/hast.1368

Bhabha, H. (1984). Of mimicry and man: The ambivalence of colonial discourse. *October, 28,* 125–133. https://doi.org/10.2307/778467

Bhabha, H. (1994). *The location of Culture.* Routledge.

Bochner, A. P. (2017). Heart of the matter: A mini-manifesto for autoethnography. *International Review of Qualitative Research, 10*(1), 67–80. https://doi.org/10.1525/irqr.2017.10.1.67

Boonzaier, F. A., & Van Schalkwyk, S. (2011). Narrative possibilities: Poor women of color and the complexities of intimate partner violence. *Violence Against Women, 17*(2), 267–286. https://doi.org/10.1177/1077801210397796

Braun, V., & Clarke, V. (2006). Using thematic analysis in psychology. *Qualitative Research in Psychology, 3*(2), 77–101. https://doi.org/10.1191/1478088706qp063oa

Braun, V., & Clarke, V. (2019). Reflecting on reflexive thematic analysis. *Qualitative Research in Sport, Exercise and Health, 11*(4), 589–597. https://doi.org/10.1080/2159676X.2019.1628806

Braun, V., & Clarke, V. (2020). One size fits all? What counts as quality practice in (reflexive) thematic analysis? *Qualitative Research in Psychology, 18*(3), 328–352. https://doi.org/10.1080/14780887.2020.1769238

Breasted, J. H. (1920). The origins of civilization. *The Scientific Monthly, 10*(2), 182–209.

Brooks, J. (1994). Chinua Achebe, The Art of Fiction No. 139. *The Paris Review.* https://www.theparisreview.org/interviews/1720/the-art-of-fiction-no-139-chinua-achebe

Byrne, D. (2022). A worked example of Braun and Clarke's approach to reflexive thematic analysis. *Quality & Quantity, 56*(3), 1391–1412. https://doi.org/10.1007/s11135-021-01182-y

Catherine Corrigall–Brown, Corrigall-Brown, C., Mabel Ho, & Ho, M. (2013). *Life history research and social movements.* https://doi.org/10.1002/9780470674871.wbespm122

Clandinin, J., D. (2022). *Engaging in narrative inquiry* (2nd ed.). Routledge.

Clarke, V., & Braun, V. (2014). Thematic analysis. In T. Teo (Ed.), *Encyclopedia of critical psychology* (pp. 1947–1952). Springer New York. https://doi.org/10.1007/978-1-4614-5583-7_311

Clifford, J. (1986). Introduction: partial truths. In *Writing culture: In the poetics and politics of anthropology* (pp. 1–26). University of California.

Collins, P. H. (1986). Learning from the outsider within: The sociological significance of black feminist thought. *Social Problems, 33*(6), S14–S32. https://doi.org/10.2307/800672

Connelly, F. M., & Clandinin, J., D. (1990). Stories of experience and narrative inquiry. *Educational Researcher, 19*(5), 2–14.

Conyers, J. L. (1997). *Africana studies: A disciplinary quest for both theory and method.* McFarland & Company Inc.

Corbie-Smith, G., Thomas, S. B., & George, D. M. M. (2002). Distrust, race, and research. *Archives of Internal Medicine, 162*(21): 2458–2463.

Counts, T. (2024). *Along the Eastern Seaboard: An exhibit focusing on the stories of African Americans along the Eastern Seaboard from Maine to Florida.* Along the Eastern Seaboard. https://alongtheeasternseadboard.omeka.net/exhibits/show/alongtheseaboard

Crenshaw, K. (1989). Demarginalizing the intersection of race and sex: A Black feminist critique of antidiscrimination doctrine, feminist theory and antiracist politics. *The University of Chicago Legal Forum, 1,* 139–167.

Crenshaw, K. (1991). Mapping the margins: Intersectionality, identity politics, and violence against women of color. *Stanford Law Review, 43*(6), 1241. https://doi.org/10.2307/1229039

Crenshaw, K. (1998). Demarginalizing the intersection of race and sex: A Black feminist critique of antidiscrimination doctrine, feminist theory, and antiracist politics. In A. Phillips (Ed.), *Feminism and Politics* (pp. 314–343). Oxford University Press. https://doi.org/10.1093/oso/9780199782063.003.0016

Creswell, J. W., & Poth, C. N. (2024). *Qualitative inquiry & research design: Choosing among five approaches* (5th ed.). Sage.

Cummings, M. S., & Roy, A. (2002). Manifestations of Afrocentricity in rap music. *Howard Journal of Communications, 13*(1), 59–76. https://doi.org/10.1080/106461702753555049

Dangermond, J., & Dangermond, L. (1969). *Environmental Systems Research Institute, Inc. (ESRI)* [Computer software]. https://www.esri.com/en-us/home

Davis, C. (2022). *Black towns & Settlements: foundation for the future.* Black Towns & Settlements: Foundation for the Future. https://storymaps.arcgis.com/stories/f33c40b9ae044f878db0fe7a4b912fb2

De Chesnay, M. (2014). *Nursing research using life history: Qualitative designs and methods in nursing.* Springer.

Denzin, N. (1992). *Symbolic interactionism and cultural studies: POLITICS of interpretation.* Blackwell.

Denzin, N., & Lincoln, Y. S. (2011). *The Sage handbook of qualitative research* (4th ed.). Sage.

Dewey, J. (1938). *Logic: The theory of inquiry.* Henry Holt & Company Inc.

Dotson, K. (2014). Conceptualizing epistemic oppression. *Social Epistemology, 28*(2), 115–138.

D'silva, M. U., Smith, S. E., Della, L. J., Potter, D. A., Rajack-Talley, T. A., & Best, L. (2016). Reflexivity and positionality in researching African-American communities: Lessons from the field. *Intercultural Communication Studies, 25*(1), 94–109.

Dumas, M. J., & Ross, K. M. (2016). "Be real Black for me": Imagining BlackCrit in Education. *Urban Education, 51*(4), 415–442. https://doi.org/10.1177/0042085916628611

Edgar, H. (2009). Biohistorical approaches to "race" in the United States: Biological distances among African Americans, European Americans, and their ancestors. *American Journal of Physical Anthropology, 139* 1, 58–67. https://doi.org/10.1002/ajpa.20961

Edwards, J. (2021). Ethical autoethnography: Is it possible? *International Journal of Qualitative Methods, 20*, 1609406921995306. https://doi.org/10.1177/1609406921995306

Egharevba, I. (2001). Researching an-'other' minority ethnic community: Reflections of a black female researcher on the intersections of race, gender and other power positions on the research process.

International Journal of Social Research Methodology, 4(3), 225–241. https://doi.org/10.1080/13645570010023760

Ejegi-Memeh, S., Berkeley, R., Bussue, D., Mafoti, W., Mohamad, A., Myrie, U., & Samuels, S. (2025). The role of Black-led community organisations in supporting Black mental health: A Black emancipatory action research project. *Ethnicity & Health*, *30*(3), 432–451. https://doi.org/10.1080/13557858.2024.2442323

Ellis, C. (2009). Autoethnography as method (review). *Biography*, *32*(2), 360–363. https://doi.org/10.1353/bio.0.0097

Etienne, M., & Leacock, E. B. (1980). *Women and colonization: Anthropological perspectives*. Bergin.

Ewuoso, C., & Hall, S. (2019). Core aspects of Ubuntu: A systematic review. *South African Journal of Bioethics and Law, 12*(2), 93–103.

Faraday, A., & Plummer, K. (1979). Doing life histories. *The Sociological Review*, *27*(4), 773–798. https://doi.org/10.1111/j.1467-954X.1979.tb00360.x

Farrell Racette, S. (2022). Kitchen tables and beads space and gesture in contemplative and creative research. In H. Igloliorte & C. Taunton (Eds.), *The Routledge companion to indigenous art histories in the United States and Canada* (pp. 85–91). Routledge. https://doi.org/10.4324/9781003014256

Few, A. L., Stephens, D. P., & Rouse-Arnett, M. (2003). Sister-to-sister talk: Transcending boundaries and challenges in qualitative research with black women. *Family Relations*, *52*(3), 205–215. https://doi.org/10.1111/j.1741-3729.2003.00205.x

Forsyth, M., Kent, L., Dinnen, S., Wallis, J., & Bose, S. (2017). Hybridity in peacebuilding and development: A critical approach. *Third World Thematics: A TWQ Journal*, *2*(4), 407–421. https://doi.org/10.1080/23802014.2017.1448717

Franz, F. (1986). *Black skin, white masks*. Pluto Place.

Fricker, M. (2007). *Epistemic injustice: Power and the ethics of knowing*. Oxford University Press.

Gani, J. K., & Khan, R. M. (2024). Positionality statements as a function of coloniality: Interrogating reflexive methodologies. *International Studies Quarterly*, *68*(2), sqae038. https://doi.org/10.1093/isq/sqae038

Gathogo, J. M. (2022). John Mbiti's Ubuntu theology: Was it rooted in his African heritage? *Studia Historiae Ecclesiasticae*, *48*(2). https://doi.org/10.25159/2412-4265/10292

Go, J. (2023). Anticolonial thought, the sociological imagination, and social science: A reply to critics. *The British Journal of Sociology*, *74*(3), 345–359. https://doi.org/10.1111/1468-4446.13025

Goffman, E. (1959). *Goffman, Erving. The presentation of self in everyday life*. Penguin Books.

Gomez, M. L., Kelly M. Ocasio, Ocasio, K., Amy Johnson Lachuk, Lachuk, A. J., Shameka N. Powell, & Powell, S. N. (2015). The "Battlefield": Life histories of two higher education staff members of color. *The Urban Review*, *47*(4), 676–695. https://doi.org/10.1007/s11256-015-0329-6

Goodson, I. (2001). The story of life history: Origins of the life history method in sociology. *Identity*, *1*(2), 129–142. https://doi.org/10.1207/S1532706XID0102_02

Goodson, I. (2012). *Developing Narrative Theory: Life histories and personal representation*. Routledge.

Goodson, I., Antikainen, A., Sikes, P., & Andrews M. (2016). *The Routledge international handbook on narrative and life history* (1st ed.). Routledge. https://doi.org/10.4324/9781315768199

Goodson, I. (2016). The story of life history. In I. Goodson, A. Antikainen, P. Sikes, & M. Andrews (Eds.), *The Routledge international handbook on narrative and life history* (1st ed., pp. 23–33). Routledge. https://doi-org.ezproxy.library.uvic.ca/10.4324/9781315768199

Goodson, I., & Sikes, P. (2016). Techniques for doing life history. In I. Goodson, A. Antikainen, P. Sikes, & M. Andrews (Eds.), *The Routledge international handbook on narrative and life history* (1st ed., pp. 72–88). Routledge. https://doi-org.ezproxy.library.uvic.ca/10.4324/9781315768199

Gousis, C., & Gill, A. K. (2023). Understanding acts of citizenship: Stories of black activism in Greece. *Citizenship Studies*, *27*(5), 605–622. https://doi.org/10.1080/13621025.2023.2237425

Griffin, R. A. (2012). I am an angry black woman: Black feminist autoethnography, voice, and resistance. *Women's Studies in Communication*, *35*(2), 138–157. https://doi.org/10.1080/07491409.2012.724524

Gulamhusein, S. (2024). Methodologically whirling. *Journal of Autoethnography*, 5(1), 7–20. https://doi.org/10.1525/joae.2024.5.1.7

Hafkin, N. J., & Bay, E. G. (1976). Introduction. In B. Edna & Nancy J. H. (Eds.), *Women in Africa: Studies in social and economic change* (pp. 1–18). Stanford University Press.

Harb, J. I., Anantharajah, K., Samuels-Wortley, K., & Qureshi, N. (2024). Back at the kitchen table: Querying feminist support in the academy. *International Feminist Journal of Politics*, 26(2), 427–446. https://doi.org/10.1080/14616742.2024.2329767

Hines, D. E. (2024). Toward black epistemological futures: Centering antiblack aggressions in educational research. *Teachers College Record: The Voice of Scholarship in Education*, 126(2), 214–222. https://doi.org/10.1177/01614681241238886

Howard, S. C. (2011). Manifestations of Nommo: Afrocentric analysis of President Barack Obama. *Journal of Black Studies*, 42(5), 737–750. https://doi.org/10.1177/0021934710372894

Huddart, D. (2006). *Homi K. Bhabha*. Routledge.

Jacobson, D., & Mustafa, N. (2019). Social identity map: A reflexivity tool for practicing explicit positionality in critical qualitative research. *International Journal of Qualitative Methods*, 18, 1609406919870075. https://doi.org/10.1177/1609406919870075

Jean-Pierre, J., Boatswain-Kyte, A., Collins, T., & Ojukwu, E. (2024). Designing afro-emancipatory qualitative research with and for Black people. *Qualitative Research*, 14687941241264458. https://doi.org/10.1177/14687941241264458

Jean-Pierre, J., & Collins, T. (2022). Penser une démarche épistémologique afroémancipatrice en recherche qualitative par, pour et avec les communautés noires. *Recherches qualitatives*, 41(1), 13. https://doi.org/10.7202/1088793ar

Jean-Pierre J., Collins, T., Agnant, K., Boatswain-Kyte, A., Herman, C., Mathews, T., Salami, B., & James, C. E. (2025). Broadening core research ethics principles: Insights from research conducted with Black communities. *Ethics & Human Research, 47*(5).

Jellema, P., Tutenel, P., Moser, B., Schoss, A.-S., Kevdzija, M., Jelić, A., & Heylighen, A. (2024, June 23). *The space between procedural and situated ethics: Reflecting on the use of existing materials in design research on children affected by stroke.* DRS2024: Boston. https://doi.org/10.21606/drs.2024.769

Kakuru, D. M., Nabirye, J., & Nassimbwa, J. (2024). Abortion as a muted reality in Uganda: Narratives of adolescent girls' agentive experiences with pregnancy termination. *Youth, 4,* 1481–1493.

Kakuru, D. M., & Paradza, G. G. (2007). Reflections on the use of the life history method in researching rural African women: Field experiences from Uganda and Zimbabwe. *Gender & Development, 15*(2), 287–297. https://doi.org/10.1080/13552070701391581

Kanogo, T. (2005). *African womanhood in Kenya, 1900–50.* Ohio University Press.

Kaplan, H., & Gangestad, S. W. (2015). Life history theory and evolutionary psychology. In D. M. Buss (Ed.), *The handbook of evolutionary psychology* (pp. 68–95). Wiley.

Karenga, M. (2014). Nommo, Kawaida, and communicative practice: Bringing good into the world. In R. L. Jackson II & E. B. Richardson (Eds.), *Understanding African American rhetoric* (2nd ed., pp. 3–22). Routledge. https://doi-org.ezproxy.library.uvic.ca/10.4324/9781315024332

Keren, A. (2022). *Fulljoy: Afrofuturism as a source of resistance, healing and joy* [Application/pdf]. https://doi.org/10.25820/ETD.006521

King, K. A. (2024). Promises and perils of positionality statements. *Annual Review of Applied Linguistics,* 1–8. https://doi.org/10.1017/S0267190524000035

Kingsman, J., & Davis, I. (2024). Reflexivity in co-constructed meanings: The impact of gender specific perspectives in the qualitative research context. *Qualitative Research Journal.* https://doi.org/10.1108/QRJ-09-2023-0144

Kohl, E., & McCutcheon, P. (2015). Kitchen table reflexivity. Negotiating positionality through everyday talk. *Gender, Place & Culture, 22*(6), 747–763. https://doi.org/10.1080/0966369X.2014.958063

Kouritzin, S. G. (2000). Bringing life to research: Life history research and ESL. *TESL Canada Journal, 17*(2), 01. https://doi.org/10.18806/tesl.v17i2.887

Ladson-Billings, G. (2021). Critical race theory—What it is not! In M. Lynn & A. D. Dixson (Eds.), *Handbook of critical race theory in education* (pp. 32–43). Routledge.

Lane, N. (2016). Bringing flesh to theory: Ethnography, black queer theory, and studying black sexualities. *Feminist Studies*, *42*(3), 632. https://doi.org/10.15767/feministstudies.42.3.0632

Lanford, M., Tierney, W. G., & Lincoln, Y. (2019). The art of life history: Novel approaches, future directions. *Qualitative Inquiry*, *25*(5), 459–463. https://doi.org/10.1177/1077800418817834

Lapadat, J. C. (2017). Ethics in autoethnography and collaborative autoethnography. *Qualitative Inquiry*, *23*(8), 589–603. https://doi. org/10.1177/1077800417704462

Leone, M., Laroche, C., & Babiarz, J. J. (2005). THE archaeology of black Americans in recent times. *Annual Review of Anthropology*, *34*, 575–598. https://doi.org/10.1146/ANNUREV.ANTHRO.34. 081804.120417

Levin, B. (2013). To know is not enough: Research knowledge and its use. *Review of Education*, *1*(1), 2–31. https://doi.org/10.1002/ rev3.3001

Luebbert, R., & Perez, A. (2016). Barriers to clinical research participation among African Americans. *Journal of Transcultural Nursing*, *27*, 456–463. https://doi.org/10.1177/1043659615575578

Lykes, M. B. (1983). Discrimination and coping in the lives of black women: Analyses of oral history data. *Journal of Social Issues*, *39*(3), 79–100. https://doi.org/10.1111/j.1540-4560.1983.tb00157.x

Magnan, M.-O., Soares, R., Bizimungu, S., & Leduc, J.-M. (2023). Between agency and systemic barriers: Pathways to medicine and health sciences among Black students with immigrant parents from the Caribbean or Sub-Saharan Africa in Quebec, Canada. *Medical Teacher*, *45*(11), 1268–1274. https://doi.org/10.1080/0142159X.2023.2215911

Mbiti, J. (1969). *African religions and philosophy*. Heinemann.

McAdams, D. P. (2008). *The life story interview*. North Western University. chrome-extension://efaidnbmnnnibpcajpcglclefindmkaj/ https://swkempowerlab.com/wp-content/uploads/2024/02/Life-Story-Interview.pdf

McArthur, J. (2022). Critical theory in a decolonial age. *Educational Philosophy and Theory*, *54*(10), 1681–1692. https://doi.org/10.108 0/00131857.2021.1934670

McGibbon, E. A., & Etowa, J. B. (2009). *Anti-racist health care practice*. Canadian Scholars' Press.

McClish-Boyd, K. (2018). *My soul looks back in wonder how I got over: Black women's narratives on spirituality, sexuality, and informal learning* [Doctoral dissertation, Kansas State University]. http:// hdl.handle. net/2097/39247

McClish-Boyd, K., & Bhattacharya, K. (2024). Methodological considerations for Endarkened narrative inquiry. *Qualitative Inquiry, 30*(7), 584–594. https://doi.org/10.1177/10778004231186565

McDougal, S. (2014). Africana studies' epistemic identity: An analysis of theory and epistemology in the discipline. *Journal of African American Studies, 18*(2), 236–250. https://doi.org/10.1007/s12111-013-9265-2

McKeever, M. (2000). Snakes and ladders: Ethical issues in conducting educational research in a postcolonial context. In H. Simons & R. Usher (Eds.), *Situated ethics in educational research* (1st ed., pp. 101–115). Routledge. https://doi-org.ezproxy.library.uvic. ca/10.4324/9780203354896

McLean, K. C. (2008). Stories of the young and the old: Personal continuity and narrative identity. *Developmental Psychology, 44*(1), 254–264. https://doi.org/10.1037/0012-1649.44.1.254

Memmi, A. (2013). *The colonizer and the colonized.* Routledge.

Mignolo, W. D. (2007). INTRODUCTION: Coloniality of power and de-colonial thinking. *Cultural Studies, 21*(2–3), 155–167. https:// doi.org/10.1080/09502380601162498

Mignolo, W. D., & Walsh, C. E. (2018). *On decoloniality: Concepts, analytics, praxis.* Duke University Press. https://doi.org/10.1515/ 9780822371779

Milton-Williams, T., & Bryan, N. (2021). Respecting a cultural continuum of black male pedagogy: Exploring the life history of a black male middle school teacher. *Urban Education, 56*(1), 32–60. https:// doi.org/10.1177/0042085916677346

Mishra, V., & Hodge, B. (1991). What is post(–)colonialism? *Textual Practice,5*(3),399–414.https://doi.org/10.1080/09502369108582124

Moore, E. (2013). Transmission and change in South African motherhood: Black mothers in three-generational Cape Town families. *Journal of Southern African Studies, 39*(1), 151–170. https://doi.org /10.1080/03057070.2013.764713

Mucina, D. D. (2011). Story as research methodology. *AlterNative: An International Journal of Indigenous Peoples*, 7(1), 1–14. https://doi.org/10.1177/117718011100700101

Myrie, R. C., Breen, A. V., & Ashbourne, L. (2022). "Finding my blackness, finding my rhythm": Music and identity development in African, Caribbean, and Black emerging adults. *Emerging Adulthood*, 10(4), 824–836. https://doi.org/10.1177/21676968211014659

Natukunda, L., Brooks, S., & Ji, J. (2019). *A simple guide to critical academic reading and writing*. Beeranga Mwesigwa Publishers.

Navarro, T., Williams, B., & Ahmad, A. (2013). Sitting at the kitchen table: Fieldnotes from women of color in anthropology: Introduction: Gender, race, and anthropological practice. *Cultural Anthropology*, 28(3), 443–463. https://doi.org/10.1111/cuan.12013

Nelson, L. (1996). Hands in the chit'lins: Notes on native anthropological research among African American women. In G. Etter-Lewis & M. Foster (Eds.), *Unrelated kin: Race and gender in women's personal narratives* (pp. 183–199). Routledge.

New York City Landmarks Preservation Commission. (2025). *Preserving significant places of black history: African American landmarks and historic districts in New York City*. Preserving Significant Places of Black History. https://storymaps.arcgis.com/stories/2e2f8343e7254e948f5a0d3699ba91fd?utm

Noxolo, P. (2017). Decolonial theory in a time of the re-colonisation of UK research. *Transactions of the Institute of British Geographers*, 42(3), 342–344. https://doi.org/10.1111/tran.12202

Osei, K. (2019). Fashioning my garden of solace: A black feminist autoethnography. *Fashion Theory*, 23(6), 733–746. https://doi.org/10.1080/1362704X.2019.1657272

Osei-Tutu, A. A. Z. (2021a). *Towards the development of African oral traditional storytelling as an inquiry framework for the study of African peoples* [Doctoral dissertation, Purdue University]. https://doi.org/10.25394/PGS.14501346.v1

Osei-Tutu, A. A. Z. (2021b). Utilizing African oral traditional storytelling to counter racist pedagogy. *Oxford Review of Education*, 14(2), 1–16.

Osei-Tutu, A. A. Z. (2023). Developing African oral traditional storytelling as a framework for studying with African peoples. *Qualitative Research*, 23(6), 1497–1514. https://doi.org/10.1177/14687941221082263

Osseo-Asare, P. (2017). *Postcolonial theory and early literacy development for 4–8 year-olds: A life history study of Ghanaian teachers* [Doctoral dissertation, The University of Sheffield]. chrome-extension://efaidnbmnnnibpcajpcglclefindmkaj/https://etheses.whiterose.ac.uk/id/eprint/18355/1/POAO-PhD%20final%20thesis-

Pabon, A. (2016). Waiting for black superman: A look at a problematic assumption. *Urban Education*, *51*(8), 915–939. https://doi.org/10.1177/0042085914553673

Pabon, A. J.-M. (2017). In hindsight and now again: Black male teachers' recollections on the suffering of black male youth in US public schools. *Race Ethnicity and Education*, *20*(6), 766–780. https://doi.org/10.1080/13613324.2016.1195359

Pierre, J. (2020). Slavery, anthropological knowledge, and the racialization of Africans. *Current Anthropology*, *61*(S22), S141–339.

Pike, K. (1967). *Language in relation to a unified theory of structure of human behavior* (2nd ed.). Mouton.

Pincock, K., & Jones, N. (2020). Challenging power dynamics and eliciting marginalized adolescent voices through qualitative methods. International Journal of Qualitative Methods, 19, 1609406920958895. https://doi.org/10.1177/1609406920958895

Plaza, D. (2006). The construction of a segmented hybrid identity among one-and-a-half-generation and second-generation Indo-Caribbean and African Caribbean Canadians. *Identity*, *6*(3), 207–229. https://doi.org/10.1207/s1532706xid0603_1

Ramdeo, J. (2025). Black women educators' stories of intersectional invisibility: Experiences of hindered careers and workplace psychological harm in school environments. *Educational Review*, *77*(2), 475–494. https://doi.org/10.1080/00131911.2023.2217358

Rebecca Sear, & Sear, R. (2020). Do human 'life history strategies' exist? *Evolution and Human Behavior*, *41*(6), 513–526. https://doi.org/10.1016/j.evolhumbehav.2020.09.004

Reed, A. (2022). The black situation: Notes on black critical theory now. *American Literary History*, *34*(1), 283–300. https://doi.org/10.1093/alh/ajac001

Reynaldo, A. (2016). AFROFUTURISM 2.0 & THE BLACK SPECULATIVE ARTS MOVEMENT: Notes on a Manifesto. *Obsidian (Raleigh, NC: 2006)*, *42*(1/2), 228–236.

Rojas, F. (2007). *From black power to black studies: How a radical social movement became an academic discipline*. John Hopkins University Press.

Roy Rosenzweig Center for History and New Media and the Corporation for Digital Scholarship. (2002). *The 911 digital archive*. The September 11 Digital Archive: Saving the Histories of September 11, 2001. https://911digitalarchive.org/

Roy Rosenzweig Center for History and New Media and the Corporation for Digital Scholarship, & George Mason University. (2008). *Omeka*. Omeka; Open-Source Web Publishing Platforms for Sharing Digital Collections and Creating Media-Rich Online Exhibits. https://omeka.org/

Roy Rosenzweig Center for History and New Media, & University of New Orleans. (2005). *Hurricane Digital Memory Bank: Collecting and Preserving the Stories of Katrina and Rita*. Hurricane Digital Memory Bank. https://hurricanearchive.org/

Runyan, A. S. (2018). *What is intersectionality and why is it important?* *Academe Magazine, 104*(6), 10–14.

Said, E. (1978). *Orientalism*. Routledge & Kegan Paul.

Sajed, A., & Seidel, T. (2023). Anticolonial connectivity and the politics of solidarity: Between home and the world. *Postcolonial Studies, 26*(1), 1–12. https://doi.org/10.1080/13688790.2023.2127652

Salami, B., Denga, B., Taylor, R., Ajayi, N., Jackson, M., Asefaw, M., & Salma, J. (2021). Access to mental health for Black youths in Alberta. *Health Promotion and Chronic Disease Prevention in Canada, 41*(9), 245–253. https://doi.org/10.24095/hpcdp.41.9.01

Samuel, M. A. (2009). On becoming a teacher: Life history research and the force-field model of teacher development. In I. Goodson, A. Antikainen, P. Sikes, & M. Andrews (Eds.), *The Routledge international handbook on narrative and life history* (pp. 1–17). https://doi.org/10.1163/9789087908584_002

Shopes, L. (2011). Oral history. In *The SAGE handbook of qualitative research* (pp. 451–465). Sage.

Siedman, I. (2006). *Interviewing as qualitative research: A guide for researchers in education and the social sciences*. Teachers College Press.

Slay, Z. M. (2023). Unmasking my truth: Autoethnography of psychological stress as a black woman in the academy. *Journal of Black Studies*, *54*(1), 3–22. https://doi.org/10.1177/00219347221134280

Smaw, E. D. (2022). Uterus collectors: The case for reproductive justice for African American, Native American, and Hispanic American female victims of eugenics programs in the United States. *Bioethics*, *36*(3), 318–327. https://doi.org/10.1111/bioe.12977

Smith, H. (2020). *Understanding the role of community in knowledge mobilisation* [Doctoral dissertation], University of York.

Smith, J. R. (2015). Unequal burdens of loss: Examining the frequency and timing of homicide deaths experienced by young Black Men across the life course. *American Journal of Public Health*, *105*(S3), S483–S490. https://doi.org/10.2105/AJPH.2014.302535

Smith, L. T. (2012). *Decolonizing methodologies: Research and Indigenous peoples* (2nd ed.). Zed Books.

Smith Lee, J. R., & Robinson, M. A. (2019). "That's My Number One Fear in Life. It's the Police": Examining young Black Men's exposures to trauma and loss resulting from police violence and police killings. *Journal of Black Psychology*, *45*(3), 143–184. https://doi.org/10.1177/0095798419865152

Sosulski, M. R., Buchanan, N. T., & Donnell, C. M. (2010). Life history and narrative analysis: Feminist methodologies contextualizing black women's experiences with severe mental illness. *The Journal of Sociology & Social Welfare*, *37*(3), 29–58.

Spooner, M. (2019). A life history of place: A future place for life histories? *Qualitative Inquiry*, *25*(5), 513–522. https://doi.org/10.1177/1077800418817840

Starks, F. D. (2022). Centering Black women's ways of knowing: A review of critical literacies research in early childhood. *Journal of Early Childhood Literacy*, *22*(3), 335–356. https://doi.org/10.1177/14687984221121156

Stitt & Happel-Parkins. (2019). "Sounds like something a white man should be doing": The shared experiences of black women engineering students. *The Journal of Negro Education*, *88*(1), 62. https://doi.org/10.7709/jnegroeducation.88.1.0062

Talal, A. (1979). Anthropology & the colonial encounter. In G. Huizer & B. Mannheim (Eds.), *The politics of anthropology: From colonialism to sexism toward a view from below* (pp. 85–96). De Gruyter Mouton. https://doi.org/10.1515/9783110806458.85

Terrefe, S. D. (2020). Afropessimism by Frank Wilderson. *The Georgia Review, 74*(4), 1047–1051.

Toliver, S. R., Jones, S. P., Jiménez, L., Player, G., Rumenapp, J. C., & Munoz, J. (2019). "This Meeting at This Tree": Reimagining the Town Hall session. *Literacy Research: Theory, Method, and Practice, 68*(1), 45–63. https://doi.org/10.1177/2381336919869021

University of South Florida. (2022). *African American burial ground & remembering project*. African American Burial Ground & Remembering Project. https://storymaps.arcgis.com/stories/7daf92f8 6fbe4a84b1427f3e4fe2bcbc?utm

Van Niekerk, T., & Boonzaier, F. (2019). The life history approach as a decolonial feminist method? Contextualising intimate partner violence in South Africa. In F. Boonzaier & T. Van Niekerk (Eds.), *Decolonial feminist community psychology* (pp. 43–57). Springer International Publishing. https://doi.org/10.1007/978-3-030-20001-5_4

Vass, G. (2017). Getting inside the insider researcher: Does race-symmetry help or hinder research? *International Journal of Research & Method in Education, 40*(2), 137–153. https://doi.org/10.1080/1743 727X.2015.1063045

Voices for Indi. (2023). *The Indi Way: How a rural community sparked a social political movement*. Scribe. https://voicesforindi.com/

Wallace, B. A. (2022). Black critical theory in action: Analyzing the specificity of (anti)blackness. *Journal of African American Studies, 26*(3), 375–392. https://doi.org/10.1007/s12111-022-09594-2

Wang, C. C., & Geale, S. K. (2015). The power of story: Narrative inquiry as a methodology in nursing research. *International Journal of Nursing Sciences, 2*(2), 195–198. https://doi.org/10.1016/j. ijnss.2015.04.014

Warren, C. A. (2021). *About centering possibilities in black education*. Teachers' College Press.

Warren, C. E., Ndwifa, C., Sripad, P., Medich, M., Njeru, A., Maranga, A., Odhiambo, G., & Abuya, T. (2017). Sowing the seeds of transformative practice to actualize women's rights to respectful maternity care: Reflections from Kenya using the consolidated framework for implementation research. *BMC Women's Health, 17*(66), 1–18.

WE ACT. (2024). *Black history, joy, hope, futures, justice—Today, tomorrow, always.* Black History & the Environmental Justice Movement. https://storymaps.arcgis.com/stories/1a110cda3df445aa9bc8cd88d15fa93d

Wekker, G. (2021). Afropessimism. *European Journal of Women's Studies, 28*(1), 86–97. https://doi.org/10.1177/1350506820971224

White, E. (2025). Fostering Ubuntu in Black adolescents: Group counseling as a pathway to advocacy. *International Journal of Group Psychotherapy, 75*(1), 245–273. https://doi.org/10.1080/00207284.2024.2429389

Williams, N. A. (2017). The Black kitchen table agreement: The power of silence during the era of Trump. *International Journal of Qualitative Studies in Education, 30*(10), 975–981. https://doi.org/10.1080/09518398.2017.1312606

Yin, R. (2016). *Qualitative research from start to finish* (2nd ed.). The Guilford Press.

Yoshihama, M., Hammock, A. C., & Horrocks, J. (2006). Intimate partner violence, welfare receipt, and health status of low-income African American women: A lifecourse analysis. *American Journal of Community Psychology, 37*(1–2), 9–20. https://doi.org/10.1007/s10464-005-9009-0

Yosso, T. J. (2005). Whose culture has capital? A critical race theory discussion of community cultural wealth. *Race Ethnicity and Education, 8*(1), 69–91. https://doi.org/10.1080/1361332052000341006

Young, R. J. (2020a). *Postcolonialism: A very short introduction.* Oxford University Press.

Young, S. (2020b). Feminist protest and the disruptive address of naked bodies. *Current writing: Text and reception in Southern Africa, 32*(2), 158–167. https://doi.org/10.1080/1013929X.2020.1795348

Young-Scaggs, S. (2021). Afrofuturism and Womanist phenomenology as resistance, resilience, and Black joy! *Review & Expositor, 118*(3), 332–342. https://doi.org/10.1177/00346373221080926

Zembylas, M. (2025). Rethinking positionality statements in research: From looking back to building solidarity. *International Journal of Research & Method in Education,* 1–13. https://doi.org/10.1080/1743727X.2025.2475762

Postscript

This book is one of the most important educational texts in Africana-qualitative research methodology to emerge in recent years. Dr. Kakuru's text is a remarkably well-organized and accessible contribution that serves as a guide to scholarly research and service and a practical teaching tool. The text succeeds in making complex methodological concepts digestible without sacrificing academic rigor, achieving that rare balance between conversational accessibility and scholarly depth. One thing that makes this work particularly compelling is its grounding in personal narrative and lived experience. Dr. Kakuru's own reflections as an experienced researcher and the transformative power of life history research create an immediate connection with readers, demonstrating her methodology's profound human dimension. This transformative personal touch elevates the text beyond mere academic instruction to become a testament to the power of storytelling in understanding the African experience.

The introduction of *Heshima* as an Afrocentric methodology is a significant theoretical advancement for the discipline. This framework, alongside the innovative concepts of *joy-centered* approaches and Afrocentric peer review, positions the work at the forefront of culturally grounded research practices. Dr. Kakuru's methodological innovations offer researchers new language and pathways for conducting culturally aligned and ethically grounded studies with people of African descent. Throughout the manuscript, Dr. Kakuru provides an impressive array of practical tools, concrete steps, and illustrative examples that transform abstract concepts into actionable research strategies. The text functions as both a curricular innovation and a reference guide, making it invaluable for students and seasoned researchers alike. The fruitful wealth of examples ensures that readers can immediately envision how to apply these methods in their own work. Perhaps most importantly, this book teaches by example. It embodies the principles it champions, serving as a living demonstration of how scholarly work can be both rigorous and accessible, both theoretically sophisticated and practically useful.

For anyone seeking to understand and implement life history methodology in research with people of African descent, this text stands as an indispensable resource. Dr. Kakuru has created not just a book, but a comprehensive educational experience that will undoubtedly shape how future researchers approach this vital work. It is a brilliant contribution to the discipline and a testament to the power of methodological innovation grounded in cultural wisdom, scholarly excellence, and social responsibility.

Dr. Serie McDougal, III

Series Editor

The Little Black Book Series

Research Methodology, Theory and Praxis

Bio

Dr. Doris Kakuru is a professor of Child and Youth Care at the University of Victoria. She is Canadian scholar of African descent, born and raised in Uganda. She holds a PhD in Social Sciences (Wageningen University, the Netherlands), a Master of Philosophy in Social Anthropology (University of Bergen, Norway), and a Bachelors (Hons) in Sociology (Makerere University, Uganda). Her research program falls in the broad area of children's geographies. She is a renowned scholar in the field of critical African girlhood studies. Her scholar-activist work aims to dismantle discriminatory and oppressive child and youth policies and practices in global contexts and critiques Eurowestern ways of knowledge creation and mobilization. Her research takes on social justice, anti-oppressive, and decolonial perspectives and sheds light on how ongoing struggles for equity are rooted in how racial and colonial legacies intersect with contemporary structures. She predominantly conducts qualitative research and utilizes the life history method. She teaches research literacy to undergraduate students and decolonial, critical, and justice-oriented theories related to child and youth care to graduate students. In 2023, Kakuru received Canada's highest academic honour as a member of the Royal Society of Canada. She is the Editor-in-Chief of the *International Journal of Child Youth and*

Family Studies. She is also an adjunct research professor at Carleton University's Institute of African Studies and a member of the Canadian Association of African Studies. The book will offer valuable insights into using the life history method to explore Black and people of African descent.

Index

Page numbers followed by "f" indicate figures; those followed by "t" indicate tables.

www.ingramcontent.com/pod-product-compliance
Lightning Source LLC
Chambersburg PA
CBHW052020030426

42335CB00026B/3216